500 FACTS
Animals

PEGASUS
www.pegasusforkids.com

© B. Jain Publishers (P) Ltd. All rights reserved. No part of this book may be reproduced, stored in a retrieval system or transmitted, in any form or by any means, mechanical, photocopying, recording or otherwise, without any prior written permission of the publisher.

Published by Kuldeep Jain for B. Jain Publishers (P) Ltd., D-157, Sector 63, Noida - 201307, U.P.
Registered office: 1921/10, Chuna Mandi, Paharganj, New Delhi-110055
Printed in India

CONTENTS

Preface 5

INTRODUCTION

Different Types of Animals 6
Birth and Life Cycle 10
Body Composition 13
Sensory Qualities 16
Communication and Movement 20
Defence and Camouflage 29
Herbivores 32
Carnivores 36
Habitats 40
Conservation and Ecosystem 43
Procreation 48

BIRDS AND REPTILES

Species, Characteristics and Habitat 51

MAMMALS

Species, Characteristics and Habitat 90

INSECTS AND CRUSTACEANS

Species, Characteristics and Habitat 124

EXTINCT ANIMALS

Details of Extinct Animals 157

PREFACE

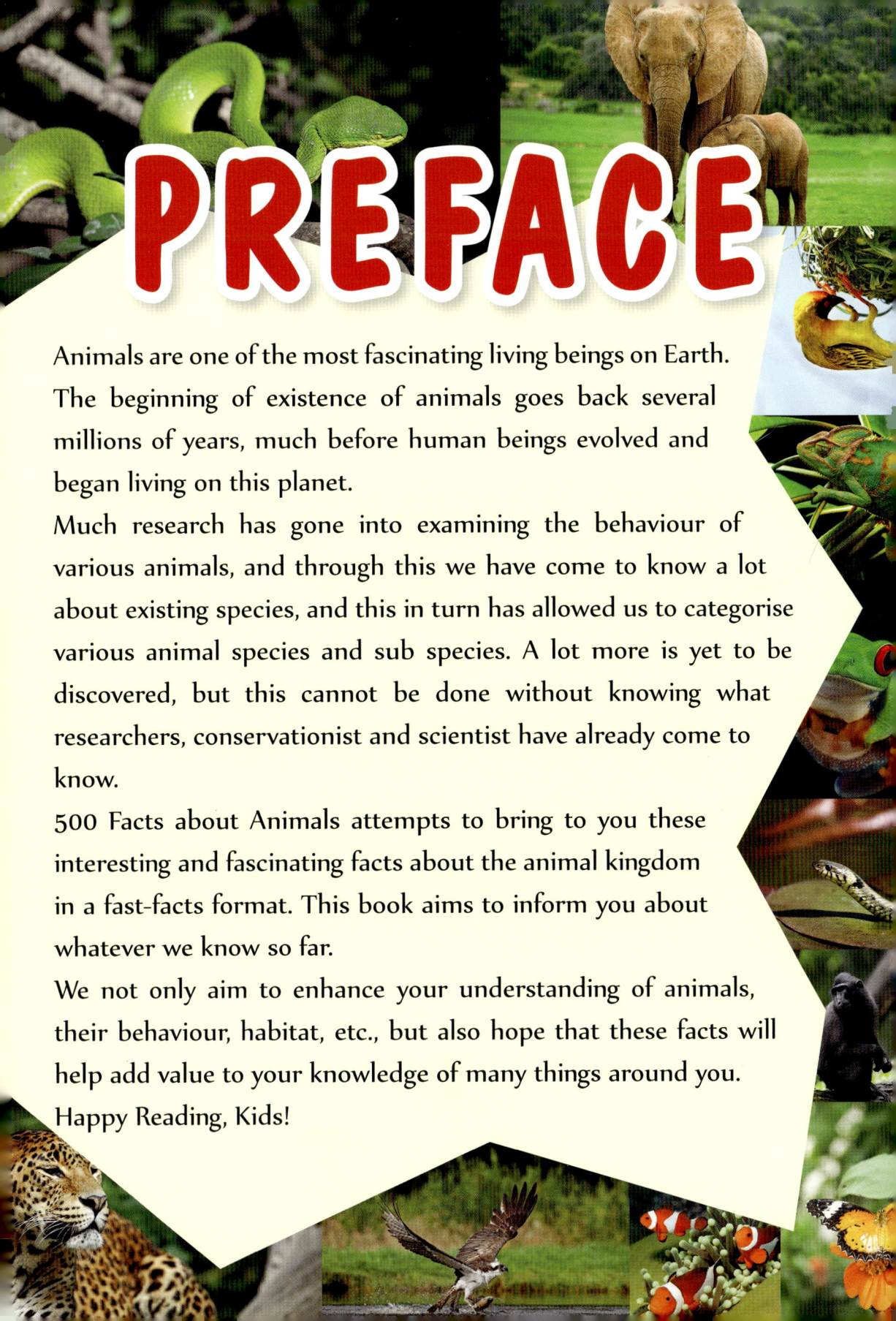

Animals are one of the most fascinating living beings on Earth. The beginning of existence of animals goes back several millions of years, much before human beings evolved and began living on this planet.

Much research has gone into examining the behaviour of various animals, and through this we have come to know a lot about existing species, and this in turn has allowed us to categorise various animal species and sub species. A lot more is yet to be discovered, but this cannot be done without knowing what researchers, conservationist and scientist have already come to know.

500 Facts about Animals attempts to bring to you these interesting and fascinating facts about the animal kingdom in a fast-facts format. This book aims to inform you about whatever we know so far.

We not only aim to enhance your understanding of animals, their behaviour, habitat, etc., but also hope that these facts will help add value to your knowledge of many things around you. Happy Reading, Kids!

INTRODUCTION

Different Types of Animals

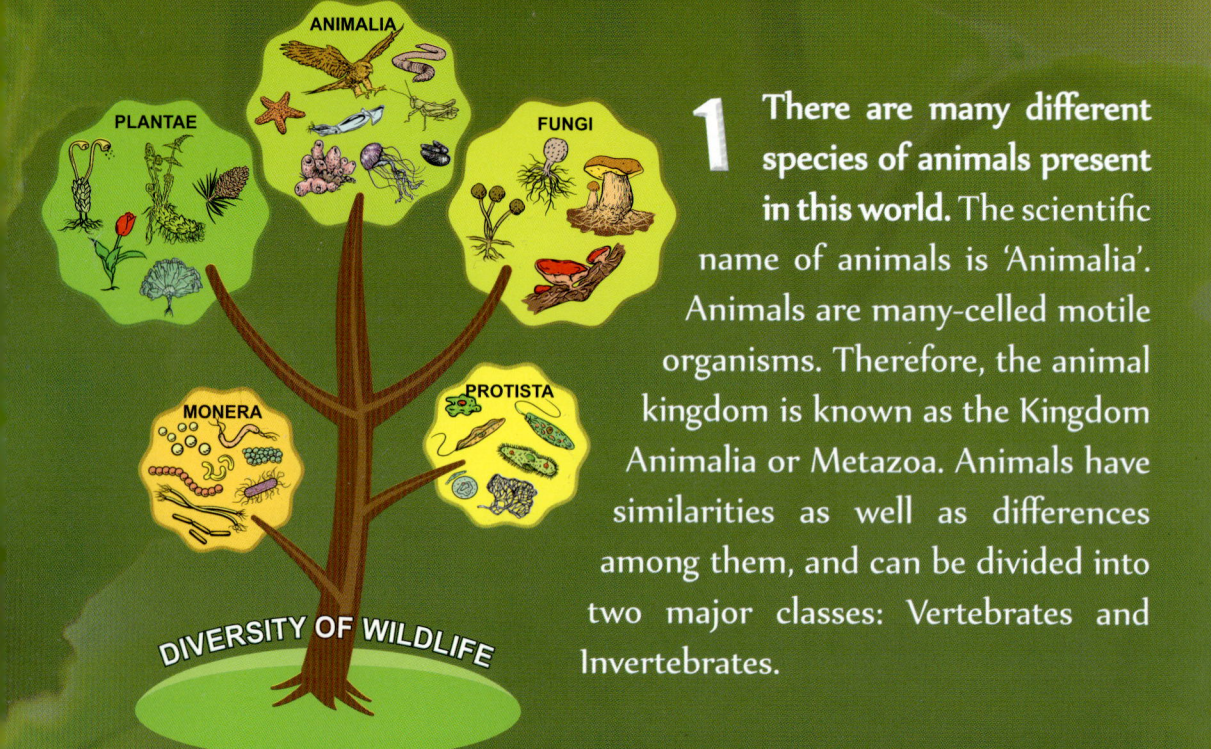

1 **There are many different species of animals present in this world.** The scientific name of animals is 'Animalia'. Animals are many-celled motile organisms. Therefore, the animal kingdom is known as the Kingdom Animalia or Metazoa. Animals have similarities as well as differences among them, and can be divided into two major classes: Vertebrates and Invertebrates.

2 **Do you know that Carolus Linnaeous was the inventor of modern scientific classification?** He was a Swedish botanist who classified more than 4,400 species of animals. This classification divides animals into Kingdom, Phylum, Class, Order, Family, Genus and Species. Therefore, it is organised in such a way that each Species belong to a Genus, each Genus belongs to a Family, each Family belongs to an Order, and so on.

DIFFERENT TYPES OF ANIMALS

3 A kingdom is made up of groups of millions of organisms. Thus, there are separate kingdoms for different creatures. The five major kingdoms are of plants, animals, fungi, prokaryotes and protoctists (type of single-celled organisms). All members of the animal kingdom have bodies made of a large numbers of cells.

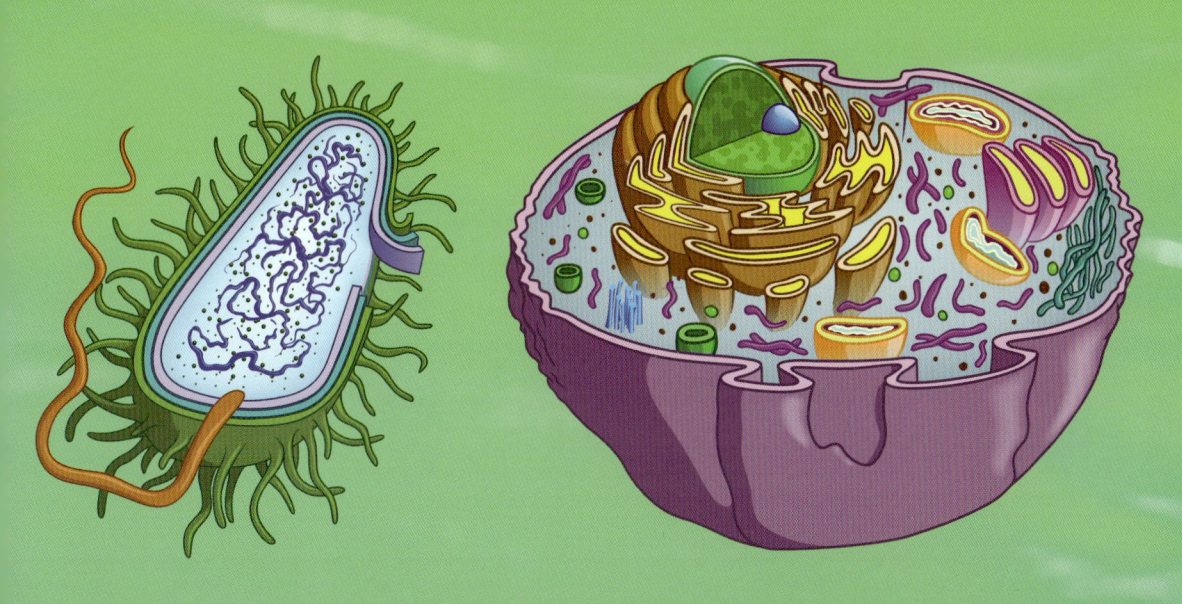

4 The animal kingdom is divided into 40 small groups known as a 'Phylum' or plural 'Phyla'. In this group, animals are classified according to their main features. The five major Phyla are: Cnidaria (invertebrates), Chordata (vertebrates), Arthropods, Molluscs and Echinoderms. Invertebrate animals with an outer skeleton and limbs, like dragonflies, crabs and spiders, belong to the Phylum Arthropoda, while cats belong to the Phylum Chordata.

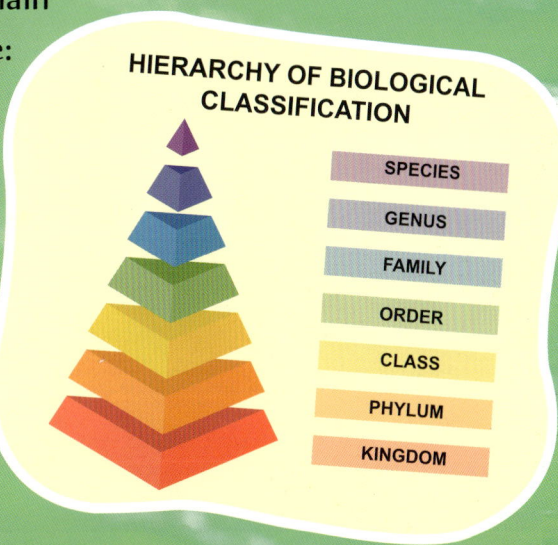

HIERARCHY OF BIOLOGICAL CLASSIFICATION

SPECIES
GENUS
FAMILY
ORDER
CLASS
PHYLUM
KINGDOM

INTRODUCTION

5 The group Phylum is again subdivided into smaller groups called 'Classes'. There are about 87 classes of organisms in the animal kingdom. The Chordata Phylum is divided into Mammalia (Mammals), Actinopyerygi (Bony Fish), Amphibia(Amphibians), Reptilia (Reptiles) and Aves (Birds). Thus, cats belong to the Class Mammalia, which includes all warm-blooded vertebrate animals which suckle their young ones.

6 Each class is broken down into small groups known as 'Orders'. A taxonomy key is used to determine in which order an organism belongs. The Class Mammalia (Mammals) is divided into Carnivora (such as cats, which are warm-blooded meat eating animals), Primate, Artiodactyla and Rodentia(rodents).

Cat family

7 Families of animals are composed of organisms that share common features and certain adaptive traits. Some families include Felidae (Cats), Canidae (Dogs), Ursidae (Bears) and Mustelidae (Weasels). The Family Felidae consists of big cats like lions and tigers as well as smaller cats like pumas, bobcats and lynxes. Humans belong to the Hominidae Family.

DIFFERENT TYPES OF ANIMALS

8 Family is subdivided into 'Genus'. It is a way to describe the generic name for an organism. There are large numbers of different Genera among animals. Each Genus comprises animals with similar features which are closely linked. For example, the Felidae (cat) Family consists of Genus including Felis (small cats and domestic cats), Panthera (tigers, leopards, jaguars and lions), and Puma (panthers and cougars).

9 The smallest group is the species. It is the lowest and most rigid level of classification of living things. The main criterion for an organism to be placed in a definite species is the ability to breed with other organisms of the same species and to give birth to young ones of the same type.

10 Vertebrates are animals that have a backbone, like reptiles, fish, birds, amphibians and mammals. Humans are mammals with a backbone, and are the most complex animals in the animal kingdom. Invertebrates do not have a backbone, like protozoa, flatworms, arachnids, insects, molluscs, and arthropods.

Birth and Life Cycle

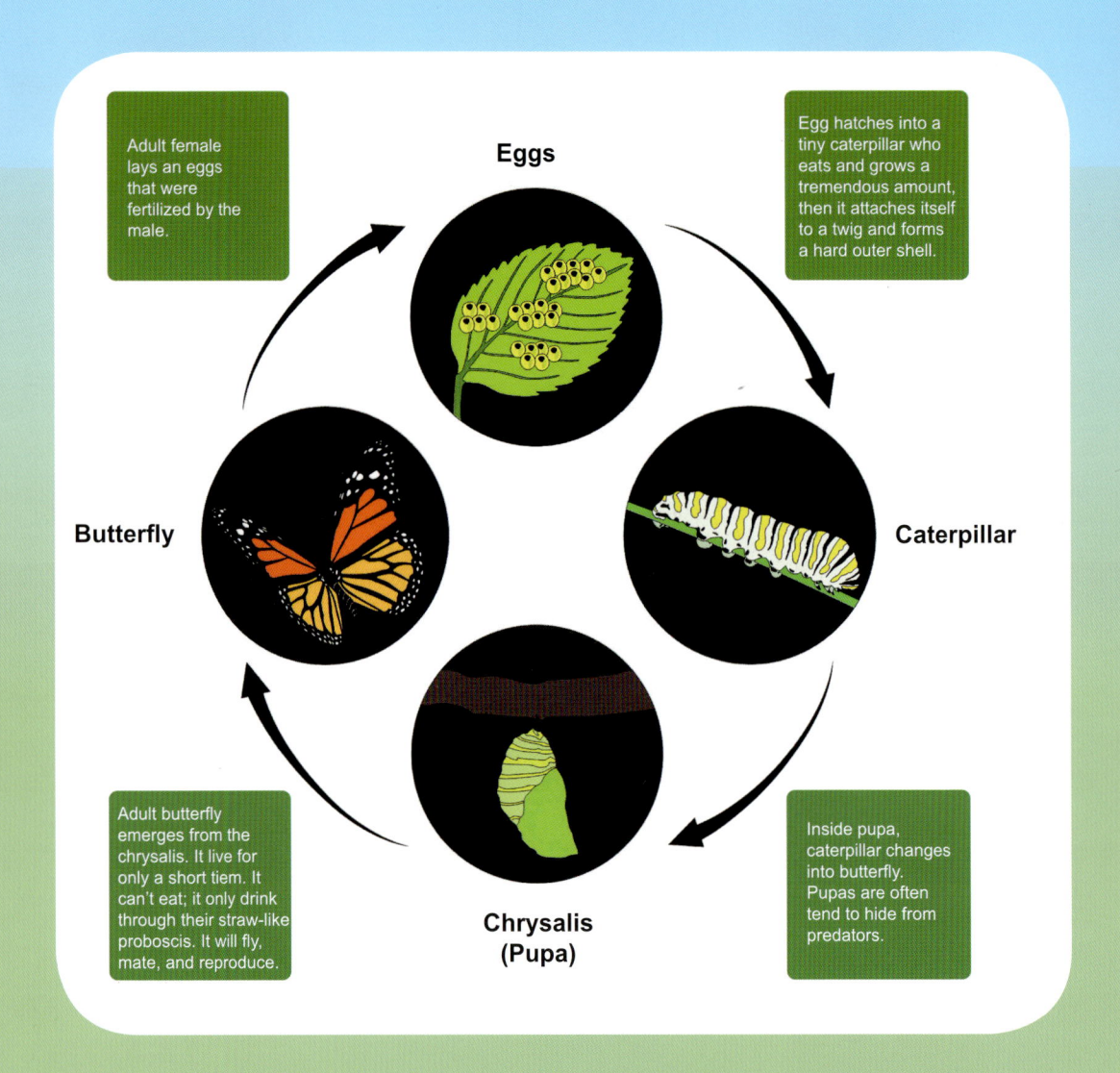

Adult female lays an eggs that were fertilized by the male.

Eggs

Egg hatches into a tiny caterpillar who eats and grows a tremendous amount, then it attaches itself to a twig and forms a hard outer shell.

Butterfly

Caterpillar

Adult butterfly emerges from the chrysalis. It live for only a short tiem. It can't eat; it only drink through their straw-like proboscis. It will fly, mate, and reproduce.

Chrysalis (Pupa)

Inside pupa, caterpillar changes into butterfly. Pupas are often tend to hide from predators.

11 As we know, some animals are born with fully developed and functioning bodies, while others are quite undeveloped at birth. Young animals are easily affected by changes in the weather, lack of food or water and predators. The young ones often survive this dangerous period by a process called metamorphosis. For instance, in the case of butterflies, larvae hatch from their eggs and later transform and become adult butterflies.

BIRTH AND LIFE CYCLE

12 **The young damselfly nymph lives in the water, where it depends for food on small animals including tadpoles and small fish.** Do you know that the nymph changes its skin many times as it grows? When it becomes ready to change into an adult, the nymph climbs out of the water and grows into its final skin to develop into a mature damselfly.

13 **The common chimpanzees depend totally on their mothers for many months after their birth.** During this period, they grow, build up their strength and learn the rules of their community. During this learning session, they indulge in a behaviour called 'play', where they chase each other, explore together, fight and learn how to talk using sounds and facial expressions.

INTRODUCTION

14 **Have you heard about baby Mexican bean beetles?** They chew their way out of individual egg shells. They come out as tiny larvae which look very different from their parents—in fact, they look like tiny caterpillars. After feeding for four to five weeks, the larvae turn into a hard-cased pupa. The creature goes through many surprising changes. After three to four weeks it turns into an adult beetle.

15 **The male Iberian midwife toad gains its name from the way it looks after its eggs.** Do you know that the male wraps 50 fertilised eggs around his back legs and carries them wherever he goes? After around three weeks he goes back to the pond and plunges the eggs in water. At that time, tadpoles hatch out of the eggs and develop into adult toads.

16 **The nest of a West African weaver bird is very long.** It is made by the male bird, and is meant partly to attract a female and partly to provide her with a safe nest. The complete nest is similar in shape to a trumpet. Did you know its unique shape helps stoptree snakes from entering the nest to steal the eggs?

Body Composition

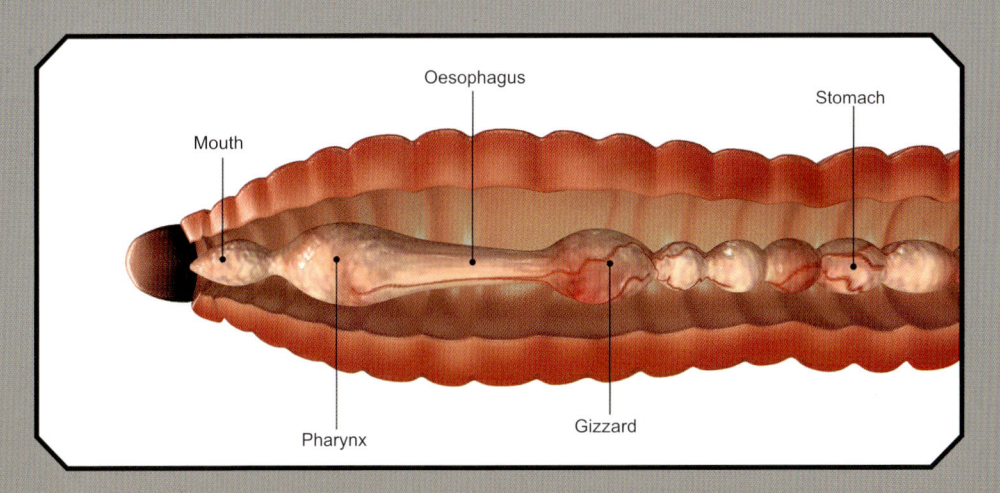

Labels: Mouth, Oesophagus, Stomach, Pharynx, Gizzard

17 **Animals have a complex body composition.** The skeleton plays a vital role as it gives shape and strength to an animal's body. The skeleton supports muscles which help in movement of bones in different directions and positions. Skeletons also act as a storage place for mineral salts. Some animals, like worms, have a solid structure along with an internal skeleton. This skeleton is mainly composed of water and is known as a 'hydrostatic' skeleton.

18 **Animals like fish, amphibians, reptiles, mammals and birds have an internal skeleton made up mainly of bones.** The skeleton of sharks and rays, however, is made of cartilage. This is a strong and rigid tissue that can bend more easily as compared to bones. In humans, this cartilage is found at the ends of bones around the joints.

INTRODUCTION

19 **One surprising fact about leeches is that they do not possess a backbone and have no solid skeleton.** Do you know how a leech maintains its shape without a skeleton? It keeps its shape by water pressure, as its body is composed of a water-filled tube along with muscles. Thus, it can move around by stretching its body.

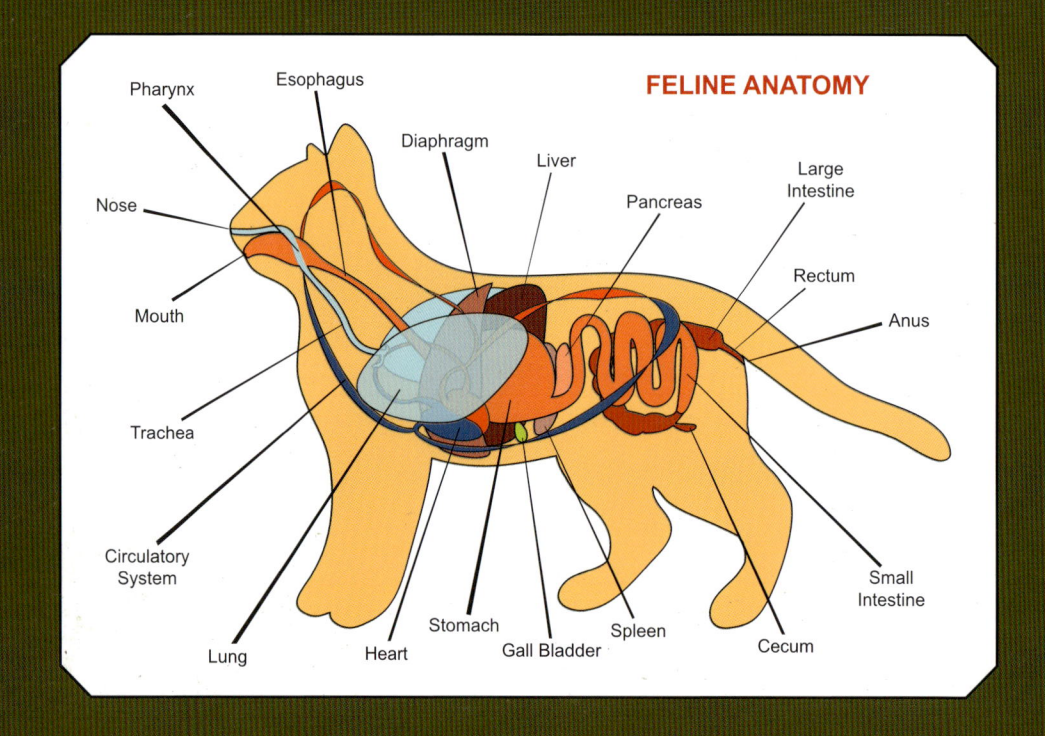

FELINE ANATOMY

Pharynx, Esophagus, Diaphragm, Liver, Pancreas, Large Intestine, Rectum, Anus, Small Intestine, Cecum, Spleen, Gall Bladder, Stomach, Heart, Lung, Circulatory System, Trachea, Mouth, Nose

20 **There are many different organs in an animal's body.** Every organ performs a special function and has a unique purpose. For example, the gills or lungs help in breathing, the gut helps in digestion, the heart pumps blood throughout the body, kidneys help in removing unwanted material from the body, muscles help in movement, and the brain makes sure that all the different systems in the body are working together.

BODY COMPOSITION

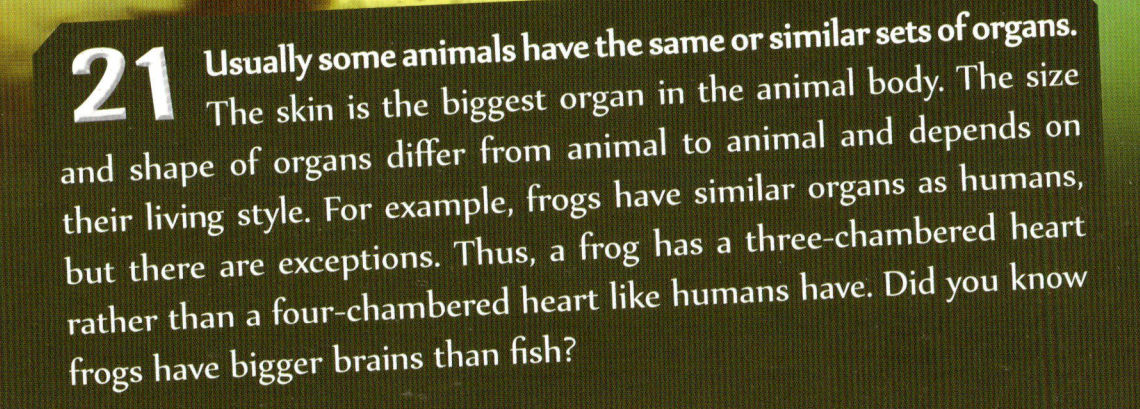

21 Usually some animals have the same or similar sets of organs. The skin is the biggest organ in the animal body. The size and shape of organs differ from animal to animal and depends on their living style. For example, frogs have similar organs as humans, but there are exceptions. Thus, a frog has a three-chambered heart rather than a four-chambered heart like humans have. Did you know frogs have bigger brains than fish?

22 The skeleton of the young Japanese giant salamander is around 0.6 m long, but as it grows into an adult it can reach a length of 1.2–1.5 m. It has a strong and flexible tail made up of more than 20 pieces of bone. With the help of this tail, it moves through water in an S-shaped movement.

23 Animals like the cockle live under the sand. They gather food from the water during high tide. The cockle's organs are designed in a way that it can move in water through the two halves of its shell. It travels very rarely and uses its fleshy foot to burrow through the sand.

Sensory Qualities

24 **Animals have different and unique sensory qualities.** Animals use these different kinds of senses to locate where they are, to find their prey and food, to predict who is attacking them, and to reach the places they want to go. Their senses are sight, smell, touch, taste and hearing which help them to create a clear picture of their world.

SENSORY QUALITIES

25 **Different animals use different senses more often than others.** For instance, the domestic pig has a special sense of smell, which is even more sensitive than that of a dog for certain odours. In Italy and France, these pigs are used to smell out small ball-like fungi known as truffles, which grow in the ground. On the other hand, sharks have a sense that allows them to detect the electrical field which is produced by the muscle movement of their prey!

26 **Insect-eating bats have a highly sensitive sense of sound, while fruit-eating bats have excellent eyesight and a sense of smell.** Their large eyes help them to find their way in the dark and their fox-like noses help them to sniff out ripe fruit or nectar.

INTRODUCTION

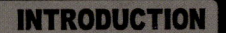

27 **The bush baby has an excellent sense of smell and sound.** Its sharp eyes help it find its way around dark forests by helping it in coping with fluctuating levels of light. Its sensitive ears help in detecting sounds, such as of a flying insect. It also has the ability to grab things quickly and can run at a high speed. These skills help it to survive.

28 **Did you know that some animals are sensitive to chemicals?** Yes, the antler-like antennae of the Indian beetle are very sensitive to chemicals. This is the reason why the beetle's perception of the world is primarily made up of patterns of smells and tastes which its antennae can easily detect.

SENSORY QUALITIES

29 Some aquatic animals can detect smell even underwater. For example, the epaulette shark has a pig-like snout with nostrils which helps it in detecting food or prey, such as sea urchins and shellfish. It can even sense a faint odour at up to three metres away. This shark uses its small, sharp front teeth to grab the food, which it then crushes with its broad and flat hind teeth.

30 The flesh fly has very efficient eyes made up of hundreds of 'mini-eyes'. The picture which is captured by this compound eye is very different from the image which is viewed by the simple eye. This means that the fly is not able to notice slow movements, but can easily see quick, sudden movements like the approach of a predator.

Communication and Movement

31 **Elephants are one of the smartest animals on Earth.** They have the biggest brain and the thickest skin among all the animals. However, they have very large, soft and sensitive ears. Did you know that when elephants flap their ears, the blood which flows through them cools down, helping them regulate their body temperature? Elephants communicate with the help of body language as well as different low frequency sounds like trumpets, rumbles, squeaks, squeals and snorts.

32 **Just like humans talk with each other to share feelings and express ideas and views, animals too talk and communicate with each other.** They use different ways to communicate and pass their messages. Sometimes, they communicate to warn others about a predator and sometimes, they make sounds to warn off their enemies. For instance, the growling of a bear or the barking of a dog are sounds of warning.

COMMUNICATION AND MOVEMENT

33 **Do you know how animals make contact with each other?** Some animals use sounds, vibrations, visual signals or smells to communicate with their group. For example, the different kinds of bird songs, a flash of colour on butterfly wings, a touch of hands between two chimpanzees and the unmistakable smell of a fox.

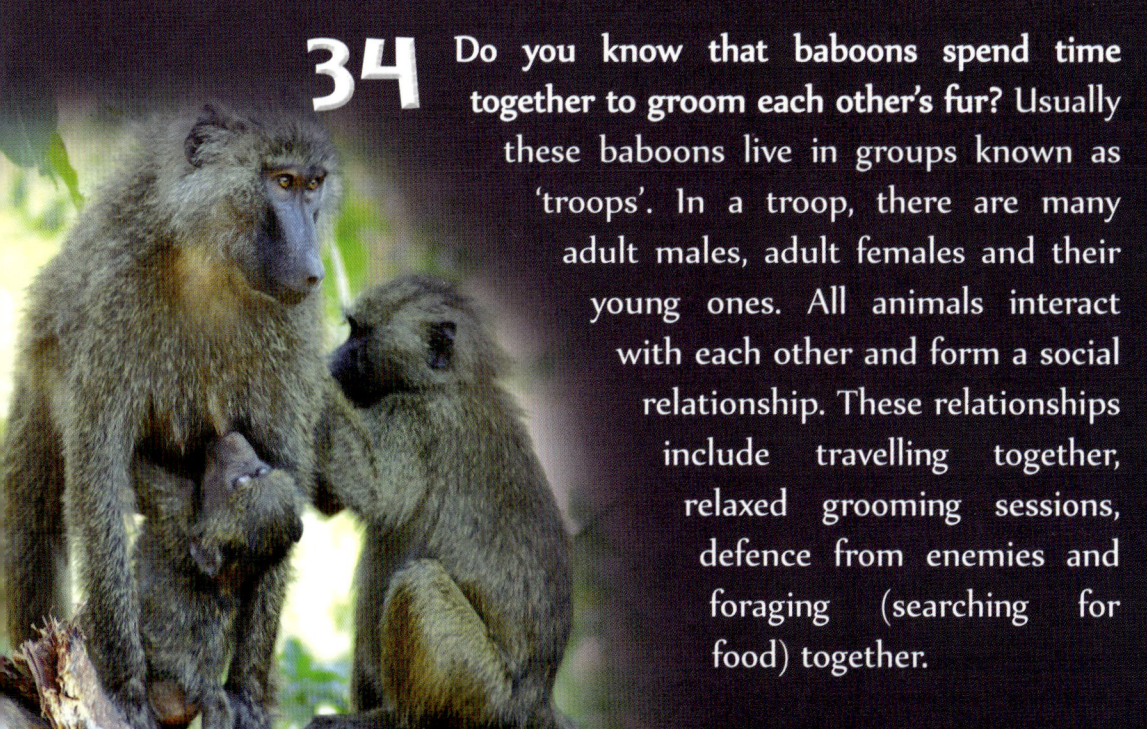

34 **Do you know that baboons spend time together to groom each other's fur?** Usually these baboons live in groups known as 'troops'. In a troop, there are many adult males, adult females and their young ones. All animals interact with each other and form a social relationship. These relationships include travelling together, relaxed grooming sessions, defence from enemies and foraging (searching for food) together.

INTRODUCTION

35 The seabirds skuas communicate with a loud barking call. While searching for food, skuas usually work together in pairs, calling out to each other. While nesting, they perform an attractive 'raised wings' display in which they hold up their wings and push their heads forward. This represents an aggressive visual signal for their enemies to keep away from their territory.

36 Do you know that smell is a key means of communication in a dog's world? Dogs talk with one another by leaving scent marks at nose level on tress, sand and posts. These smelling habits of animals are very useful for them as they make territorial boundaries which last for many days.

COMMUNICATION AND MOVEMENT

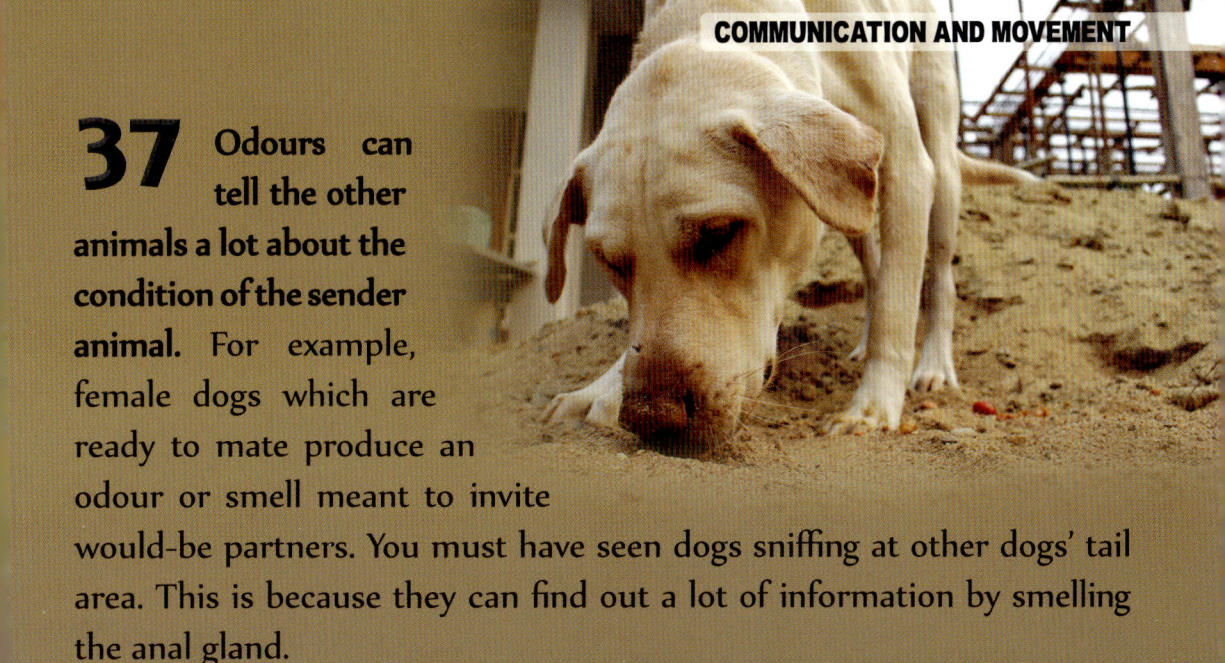

37 Odours can tell the other animals a lot about the condition of the sender animal. For example, female dogs which are ready to mate produce an odour or smell meant to invite would-be partners. You must have seen dogs sniffing at other dogs' tail area. This is because they can find out a lot of information by smelling the anal gland.

38 Do you know how wild rabbits communicate? They make short range calls to each other inside their burrows! As male rabbits have many female breeding partners, they rub their chin gland against each female to leave a scent mark on her body. This lets other male rabbits know that the female rabbits have already mated. The male also marks its boundaries with droppings to warn other males to remain away from its territory.

INTRODUCTION

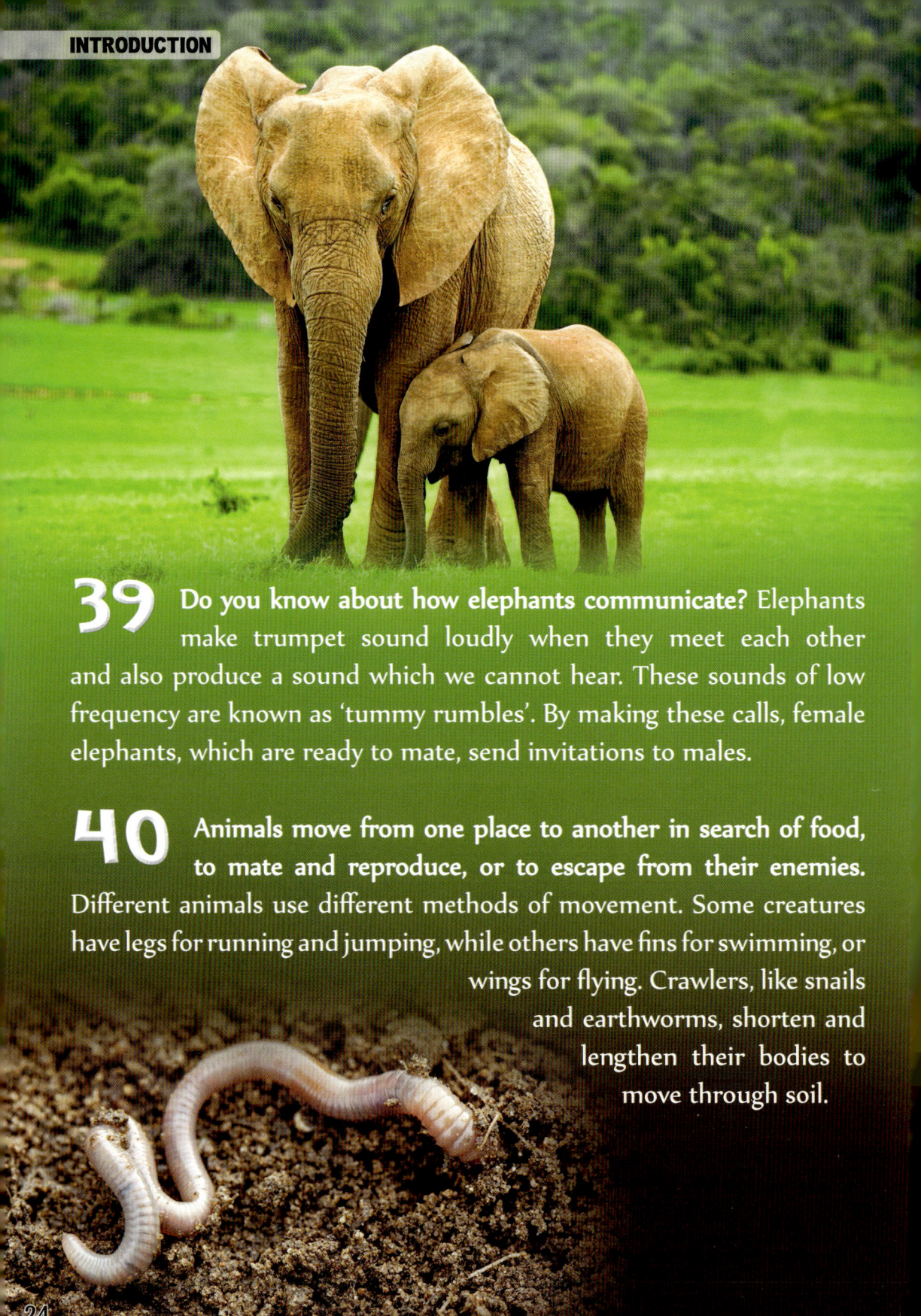

39 Do you know about how elephants communicate? Elephants make trumpet sound loudly when they meet each other and also produce a sound which we cannot hear. These sounds of low frequency are known as 'tummy rumbles'. By making these calls, female elephants, which are ready to mate, send invitations to males.

40 Animals move from one place to another in search of food, to mate and reproduce, or to escape from their enemies. Different animals use different methods of movement. Some creatures have legs for running and jumping, while others have fins for swimming, or wings for flying. Crawlers, like snails and earthworms, shorten and lengthen their bodies to move through soil.

COMMUNICATION AND MOVEMENT

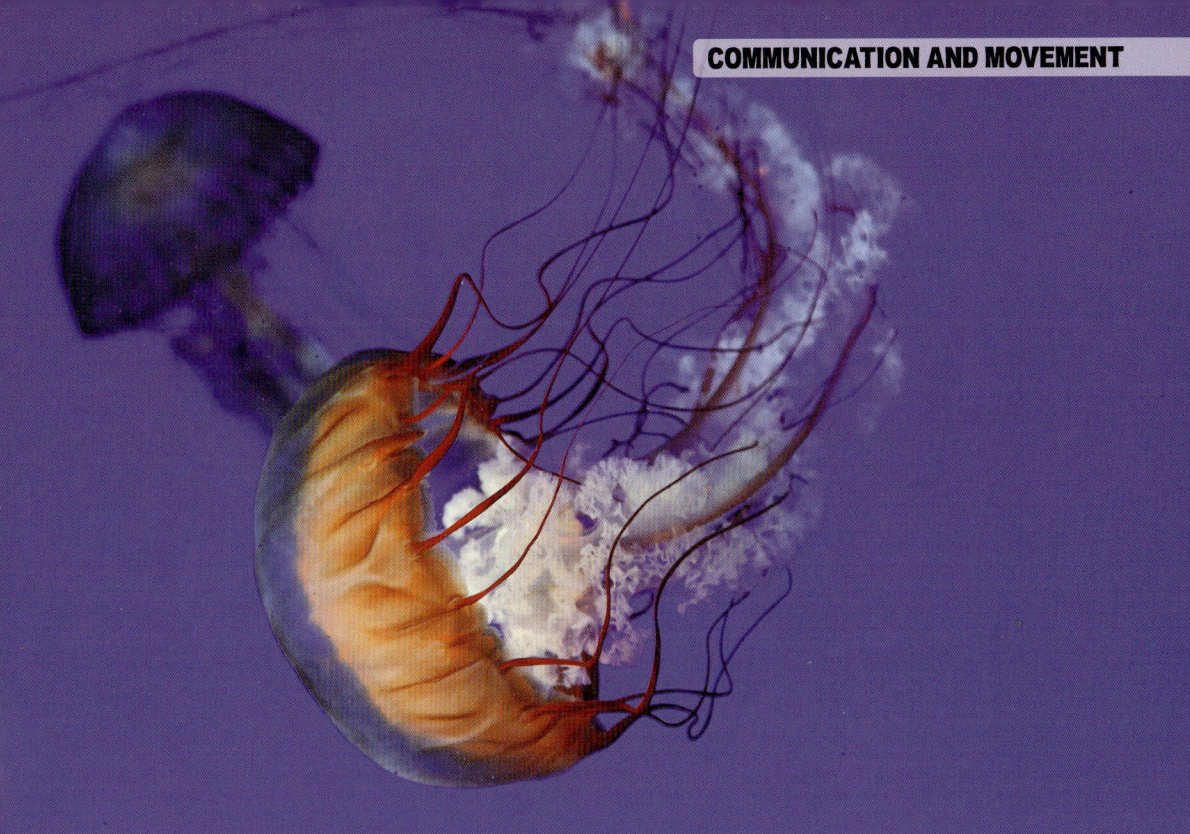

41 **Animals known as 'drifters' move very gradually.** Rather than making much of an effort themselves, they tend to take advantage of any movement which occurs in their surrounding environment. For instance, sea drifters float near the surface of the water and move along with the waves, while some small insects are carried or taken away by the currents of air.

42 Do you know that domestic cats can jump and pounce to great heights? They do not need to hunt for their food, since they are domesticated. However, they still have excellent eyesight, and the reflexes of predatory animals, and are able to pounce and land with great accuracy.

INTRODUCTION

43 The dogfish is an aquatic animal, like sharks, and moves in water by making S-shaped waves using its body. This movement begins from its head, as the fish swings from side to side. This results in a slight push which makes its body move in the forward direction, before rippling down the body to the tail.

44 Some lizards like geckos have special scaly skin on their feet, which is similar to sucker pods. These ridges are covered in millions of tiny hairs. This allows them to grip onto almost any surface easily. Thus, geckos can move in upright direction along tree trunks and even on ceilings in houses.

COMMUNICATION AND MOVEMENT

45 **The bird named mallard duck uses its light, flexible wings to move across the sky.** Its wings are curved slightly from front to back, in a shape similar to aircraft wings. Due to this shape, the bird can easily move upward through the air by flapping its wings.

46 **Do you know about the green tree frog of Australia?** It moves its body from side to side in order to go from one place to another. The reason behind this strange movement is that the front and rear limbs on each side of its body move together as pair. Its toes have sticky pads at the ends which help it to get a strong grip, climbing trees or walking on leaf surfaces easily.

INTRODUCTION

47 The green anaconda moves by crawling because, like all snakes, it has no legs and moves on its ribs. The body of the snake can easily curve and bend around objects like stones and plants. The pressure produced by its muscular movement passes back along the body and exerts this pressure against the stones and plants, enabling it to crawl forward.

Defence and Camouflage

48 **Most animals are prone to danger of being attacked by other large animals that want to eat them.** To protect themselves, some animals hide, keep very still, or run away as quickly as they can. Some others use different kinds of protection, such as sharp spines, hard shells or tough scales which act as a protective cover that protects them from attack. For instance, the porcupine has sharp quills on its back.

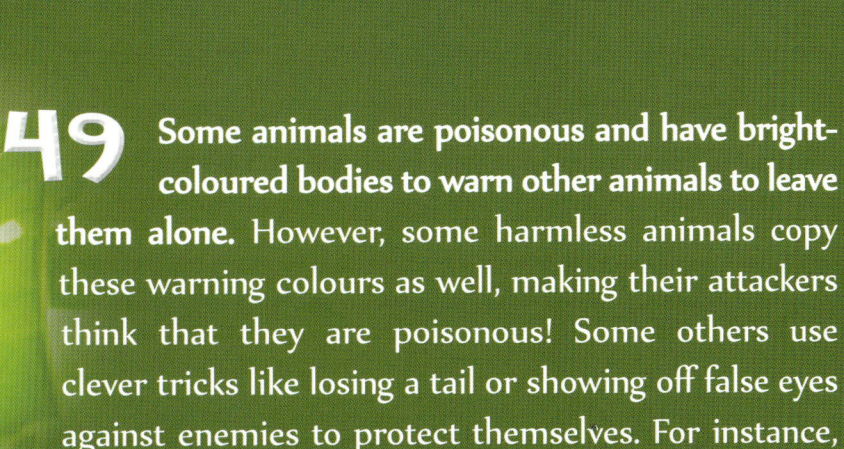

49 **Some animals are poisonous and have bright-coloured bodies to warn other animals to leave them alone.** However, some harmless animals copy these warning colours as well, making their attackers think that they are poisonous! Some others use clever tricks like losing a tail or showing off false eyes against enemies to protect themselves. For instance, birds are less likely to attack caterpillars that have fake eye spots on their body.

50 **The European grass snake first tries to hide from predators, but if that fails, it lies on its back and opens its mouth pretending to be dead!** Predators tend to try to catch moving prey, so by playing dead, the snake actually has a better chance of living. As soon as the danger passes, the snake comes 'back to life' and slithers away.

INTRODUCTION

51 **The underwater world is just as dangerous as land.** Did you know that the clown fish escapes from predators by hiding among the lethal tentacles of the sea anemone? Other fish and sea creatures would be killed immediately by the anemone's stinging tentacles, but the clown fish has a special covering of slime on its body which protects it.

52 **Do you know which animal has a coat of armour?** Armadillos are covered by armour composed of bony body plates. This is a hard, rigid covering which protects the head, tail, shoulders and hips of the animal. When they face a dangerous enemy, they pull in their feet and roll up like a ball to protect their soft undersides.

DEFENCE AND CAMOUFLAGE

53 Do you know that poison dart frogs produce some of the powerful poisons in the world in their skin? They are very poisonous because their enemies, like snakes and spiders, would not be hurt or killed by weaker poisons. These frogs have dark-coloured skin to warn their enemies and also to defend their boundaries from other males during their mating time.

54 Animals which move slowly, like hedgehogs, depend on body armour for protection. Usually, when a hedgehog rolls up into a tight ball, its coat of sharp spines protects its soft body from any dangerous predators. When the hedgehog is alarmed, it even raises the spines present on its upper body so that they point in all directions.

55 Do you know that the porcupine fish has spines present all over its body to protect itself? It has yet another defence mechanism. By swallowing air or water, the fish swells up like a balloon, making it even more difficult for a predator to swallow it. Since it has spines on each scale, these stick out when the fish is inflated, hurting the enemy even more.

Herbivores

56 The easiest and simplest foods, which an animal can find in nature, are trees, bushes, grasses and herbs. These are present in large quantities on land. However, some plants have leaves laced with poison or thorny stems to protect themselves from plant eaters.

HERBIVORES

57 **Plants have tough cell walls which makes them difficult for animals to digest.** However, there are microbes present in the guts of animals like green turtles, manatees and horses which help them to break down such food. The gut or the digestive tract is very long and allows the animal to extract as much nutrition from the plant as possible.

58 **Animals which eat only plants are known as Herbivores.** Do you know why horses take a lot of time to eat? This is because horses are herbivorous and eat stems, leaves and grasses which has very low energy content. Thus, horses need larger amounts of these foods to gain high energy. They chew the grasses using their molar teeth and then the food is broken down by fermentation.

INTRODUCTION

59

The shield bug beetle uses its efficient mouthparts to suck juice from plants. Often, shield bugs are also known as 'stink bugs' because of the bad odour they release when disturbed. The bug is very bright in colour which warns birds and other predators that it has a foul taste.

60

Do you know what caterpillars really are? They are the 'feeding stage' in a butterfly or moth's life cycle, when they eat almost constantly. While most caterpillars are herbivores and eat plant material, some are known to eat insects as well. For farmers, most caterpillars are pests that damage their crops by eating them.

HERBIVORES

61 **Do you know that the koala is not a bear but a marsupial?** Koalas have a specialised diet which contains mainly low protein and high-fibre eucalyptus leaves. A koala eats about 500 grams of food per day. Since this diet is not sufficient for the koala and does not give much energy, it moves slowly to avoid tiring, and sleeps for close to 18 hours every day.

62

The skull of the North American beaver has a pair of large front teeth. The beaver uses its teeth to strip and feed on tree bark, which is its main diet. Just like other rodents, the beaver's teeth also continuously grow, but they are worn away by regular gnawing.

Carnivores

63 **Animals that eat meat and flesh are known as Carnivores.** Meat-eating animals have distinct meal times, unlike plant eaters, who keep on feeding almost continuously. The availability of a meal depends upon how easily the prey is caught and time taken to eat it.

64 **Most meat eaters have specialised tools to capture and consume their prey.** For example, big cats have strong, mature canine teeth for grasping hold of their prey and unique cheek teeth for tearing up meat. In the oceans, sharks have pointed teeth to grab slippery squid and fish, while its triangle-shaped teeth help in cutting through flesh and blubber.

CARNIVORES

65 Do you know that the black aye-aye lemur found on the islands of Madagascar uses its long middle finger to catch its food? Just like woodpeckers go through wood to reach their prey, the aye-aye picks out wood-boring beetles that make holes in tree branches. The sharp curved claw at the top of its middle finger is used to hook the grubs up and pull them out.

66 **The sandfish lives on land, in hot and dry deserts.** During the early morning and late afternoon, it comes out of its burrows in search of food, which includes insects and small reptiles. It stays mostly above the ground to regulate its body temperature and to digest its food easily.

INTRODUCTION

67 Osprey is a fish-hawk which feeds on the fish in lakes or rivers along the coast. It snatches up fish which are swimming near the water's surface. It usually eats its prey at a specific point or in its nest, using its knife-like beak to tear off the flesh.

68 The ornate horned toad of South America is well-known as a 'sit-and-wait' feeder. This means that it hides among the fallen leaves of the forest floor and waits for its prey to come in front of it. As soon as a large insect, frog or mouse comes by, the toad opens up its huge mouth quickly and grabs its prey.

CARNIVORES

69

Have you heard of a fly that eats dangerous spiders? The female little-headed fly lays her eggs on the bodies of tarantula spiders. After sometime, when maggots hatch out, they burrow into the spider's body from all sides. Thus, the maggots always have fresh meat which provides them the nutrients, which they need to grow, until they emerge as new adult flies.

70 **The archerfish is found in tropical mangrove swamps in southern Asia and Australasia.** It is well-known for being able to spit exactly at targets at distances of more than 1 metre. It uses this skill to throw drops of water at insects and spiders, to make them fall down swamp-side branches. It also snatches up low flying insects which are passing by.

Habitats

71 **The world is a huge home for all living beings and organisms.** Each continent of the world has its own special and unique kinds of animals and habitats. Animals which travel by sea or air between continents like seals or birds are called migrants. They move from one place to another according to the changing seasons, based on where enough food is available.

72 **Some animals are only found in a few places on earth.** The duck-billed platypus is an egg-laying animal found in Australia. These primitive mammals are only found here as they are isolated and cut off from other continents. The Bhutan glory butterfly lives in the mountain forests of Thailand, Bhutan, and India, where the climate is cold and harsh.

HABITATS

73
Do you know that the greatest variety of marsupials is found on the island continent of Australia? The largest of the marsupial meat-eaters is the Tasmanian devil. It must eat a lot of food in order to survive, often preying on lambs, chickens and also scavenging for dead carcasses. It has powerful jaws that can tear off large parts of the prey, including bones and fur.

74 Different animals are adapted to different habitats or places in which they live. For example, the Arctic fox keeps itself warm in the icy weather by growing a thick, double-layered winter coat. This heavy coat protects it from the icy winds by trapping a layer of air close to the skin.

75 The Arctic is a huge frozen sea surrounded by land. Animals in the frigid polar region have to keep themselves warm in order to survive. The walrus is one such animal that lives in the Arctic. It keeps out the cold thanks to a thick layer of fat under its skin, known as blubber.

INTRODUCTION

76 **Do you know that European mole is adapted to a life underground?** Its well-developed front paws and large claws are adapted for digging tunnels inside the soil. It does not depend much on its eyesight as it has small eyes which are sensitive to changes in light levels. Instead, its snout is very sensitive and can easily pickout the smells of prey such as earthworms and insect larvae.

77 **Mountain goats are known scientifically as 'goat antelopes' which live on alpine meadows where they mostly feed on mountain grasses.** Their hooves have a strong grip which allows them to hide easily from their predators by clambering onto narrow mountain ranges. Both male and female goats carry a pair of horns that has a slight backward curve.

78 **The merlin, usually found in northern America and Eurasia during summer, is one of the top predators in the mountain regions.** It prefers to hunt in the open, low and rough vegetation in the foothills. During winter, it leaves the mountains and moves to milder coastal regions to the south and southwest.

Conservation and Ecosystem

79 **Animals play a key role in balancing our ecosystem.** Some steps to ensure their protection must be taken to protect the animal life. Unfortunately, some species have become the victims of deforestation, excessive hunting or expanding human pollution, but others have been saved from extinction because of our growing awareness of the hazards they face.

80 **Some ways in which conservation is helpful for protecting the animal kingdom are:** deep monitoring of endangered species, a strong effort to reduce pollution and protection of threatened environments. The scope of conservation work does not lie only in protection of habitat of endangered species, but also in altering the ways humans live, to decrease our harmful effects on other animals.

INTRODUCTION

81 Conservationists want industries to use resources, such as glass and paper, which are reusable in order to replace destroyed forests, and to restrict fishing to varieties which are quick to reproduce. Many governments are strictly motivating people to be fuel conscious while using electricity or petrol, and set heavy fines on industries for excessive generation of pollution.

82 Do you know that pollution which originates in one place can affect plants and animals which are thousands of kilometres away, even in another part of the world? At Chernobyl, Ukraine, in 1986 a nuclear reactor exploded. The radioactive fallout reached as far as Lapland. The semi-domestic reindeer of this place which then fed on contaminated lichens became victims of radioactivity and their meat was banned for human consumption.

83 The golden lion tamarins are some of the most closely monitored animals on Earth. Their number had decreased to less than 100 in 1980. The reason behind their decline was the growing poaching and trade in exotic animals. But due to a successful captive breeding programme, their numbers have grown and are now once more present in the wild.

CONSERVATION AND ECOSYSTEM

84 Did you know that the leopard is the most adaptable and widely classified big cat? Unfortunately, their numbers are shrinking rapidly, as they are losing their habitat, which is being converted to farmland. Only a few scattered populations exist today in Africa and Asia, where they were once very common.

85 The habitat of coral reefs provides an amazing home to a variety of marine species. However, coral is used to make jewellery and ornaments in South East Asia and the Caribbean, which poses a major threat to the existence of these reefs. If the reefs are lost, a large number of marine species will also lose their habitat. Thus, many countries have banned the collection, sale and export of coral to protect this precious habitat.

86 Some people use huge fishing boats in the ocean to set drift nets which are several miles long and float near the water surface. These invisible floating nets are meant to catch fish, but often trap and drown dolphins, whales, seals and sea turtles. To prevent this, the United Nations has now banned the use of long drift nets for fishing so that these unnecessary deaths do not happen.

INTRODUCTION

87 **All animals live together in an ecosystem, where some live together in harmony and some cause each other harm.** The study of such relationships is known as ecology. All animals are dependent on each other and cannot live alone as they depend on plants or other animals for food or protection.

88 **Some animals are a source of food for other animals.** This dependency for food can be of two kinds. The first is the food chain, where smaller animals are eaten up by larger animals. The other is the food web, composed of complex networks of animals that eat more than one type of food.

89 **Have you heard about the clever cuckoo bird?** They have a unique way of making sure their babies survive. Instead of making their own nest to hatch their eggs the cuckoo waits for other birds to lay eggs. They distract the bird, throw away her eggs, and replace it with the cuckoo's egg. Thus, the other bird actually hatches the cuckoo's egg unknowingly!

CONSERVATION AND ECOSYSTEM

90 The hermit crab and sea anemone live together in a relationship in which they both benefit. The sea anemone stays on the hermit crab's back, moving around wherever the crab goes, and thus feeding in a variety of places. In return, the stinging tentacles of the sea anemone cover the body of hermit crab, which protects it from attacks.

91 There is a strong relationship between animals and plants. For example, when tiny aphids make their home on a pistachio tree, the tree creates a protective casing known as a 'gall' around the insects. The insects receive a slow supply of food from the tree, and in return they help to spread the tree's seeds far and wide.

92 Animals depend on each other for a number of reasons, such as for feeding, through the food chain, or for protection against larger predators. Different animals may be the predators at different levels of the food chain. For example, the great white shark is at the top of the marine food chain as it is rarely eaten. Next are seals, sea lions and large fish on which the shark feeds. These creatures eat smaller fish, which eat shrimps, which feed on plankton.

Procreation

93 All animals reproduce in order to create more creatures just like themselves. This ensures that the species does not die out. Thus, during the mating season, different animals display different ways of attracting a mate. Some creatures puff themselves out to look larger, while others show attractive plumage, or defeat the other males in the area to get a mate. Some make special mating calls or release certain scents to let the others know that they are ready to mate.

94 Some animals reproduce sexually while others reproduce asexually. In sexual reproduction, two adults breed together to produce their young ones. In this form of reproduction animals need to meet and pair up with a partner. In asexual reproduction, there is no need for two partners, as the animal can breed without a partner by creating exact copies of themselves.

PROCREATION

95 **Do you know that during mating season the competition between the bull (male) elephants to mate with a female becomes very intense?** Full of excitement, bulls of similar size and power fight together until one of them withdraws from the contest. Whichever bull wins, has the right to reply to the mating calls of a female.

96 **Often, the males of the species are larger and more colourful than the females.** For instance, the male finch is more decorative than the female. This is because the males must use their size and beauty to try and attract a mate. On the other hand, the females have to try to avoid unwanted attention from predators when caring for her young. Thus, their appearance has a biological purpose.

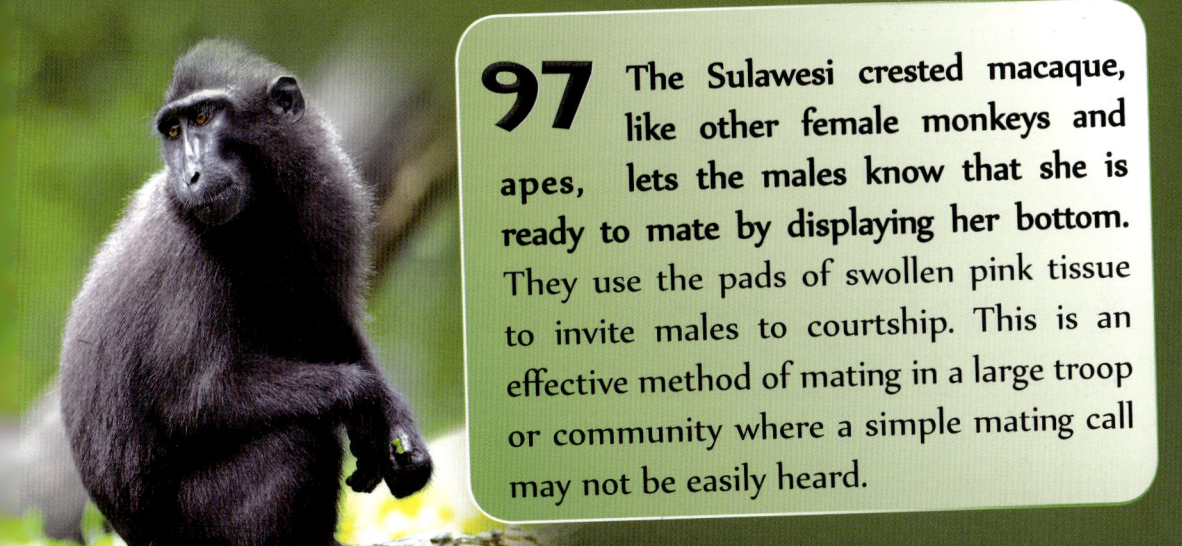

97 **The Sulawesi crested macaque, like other female monkeys and apes, lets the males know that she is ready to mate by displaying her bottom.** They use the pads of swollen pink tissue to invite males to courtship. This is an effective method of mating in a large troop or community where a simple mating call may not be easily heard.

INTRODUCTION

98 The sweet oil butterflies are brought together by a special smell generated during courtship. This process is known as **assembling**. The female releases chemicals to produce a strong scent that captures the attention of males who are keen for mating. Once they pair up, the butterflies breed together on a plant which provides them with food.

99 Do you know that the male common toad makes a distinctive mating call to attract female toads from the same species? Once a female toad is attracted, the male holds on to her in a tightmating embrace. The unique pads of rough skin on the toad's thumbs allow them to grip the females tight, despite her slippery skin.

100 Did you know that male and female tigers are different in appearance? Female tigers first come in to season when they are around two and half years of age, but do not become sexually mature until they are three or four years old. They usually become pregnant or rear cubs for the next 15 years. For males, sexual maturity occurs at approximately four to five years of age.

BIRDS AND REPTILES

Species, Characteristics and Habitat

101 **Birds are a group of warm blooded vertebrates.** While all birds have the ability to fly, some of them don't fly. Birds are covered by feathers, lay eggs, have lightweight bodies but strong skeletons, and have toothless, beaked jaws. There are as many as 8,000 species of birds in existence today.

102 **Did you know that birds are also known as avian dinosaurs?** The last surviving group of dinosaurs is birds, who evolved from their feathered ancestors. Around 100 million years ago, the first true birds appeared during the Cretaceous Period. Birds like the archaeopteryx, which were early 'stem-birds', were not capable of fully-powered flight.

103 **As most birds fly, their bodies need to be as light as possible.** Bones of the birds are hollow, making them light, and have fused struts to provide necessary strength. In order to provide power for the flight, birds' chest muscles are very strong, and are anchored to the sternum of the breast bone.

BIRDS AND REPTILES

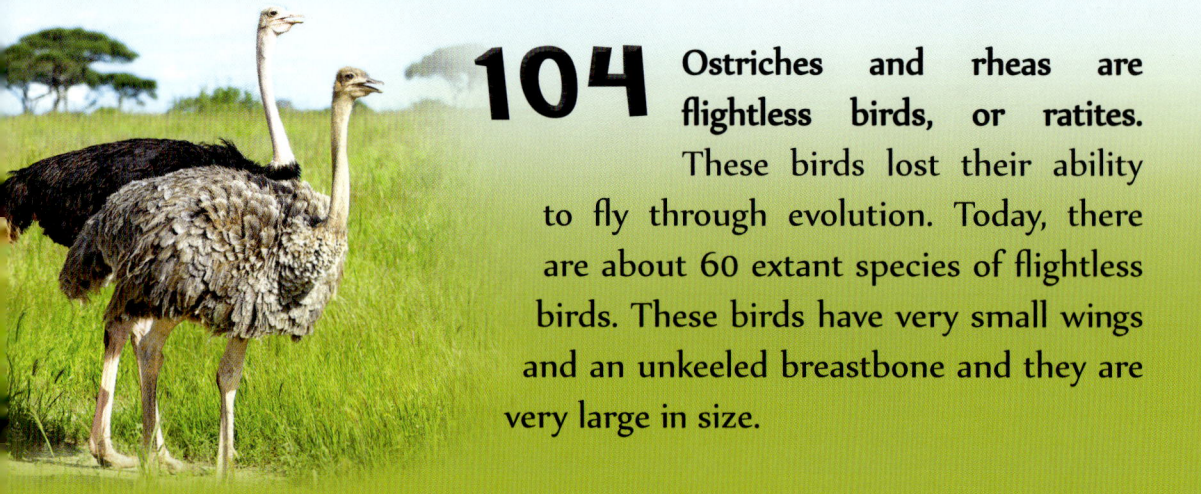

104 Ostriches and rheas are flightless birds, or ratites. These birds lost their ability to fly through evolution. Today, there are about 60 extant species of flightless birds. These birds have very small wings and an unkeeled breastbone and they are very large in size.

105 Kiwis have an excellent sense of smell, which they use to detect food. Their nostrils are placed at the tip of the upper beak, which is a very rare feature in birds. Kiwis are relatives of the recently extinct Moa, which was about three metres long. Kiwis reside in New Zealand and there are now only three living species of these birds.

106 Did you know that a female kiwi is larger in size than a male kiwi? A female kiwi lays white eggs of a very large and elongated size as compared with her own size and they weigh about 450 grams. It is the male kiwi who incubates the eggs, which take around 75 to 77 days to hatch.

SPECIES, CHARACTERISTICS AND HABITAT

107 **The ostrich is the largest bird in the world.** The weight of an adult male is about 150 kilograms, and it is nearly 2.5 metres long. Ostriches can run at a speed of 97 km/h and lay the largest eggs in the world. They generally live in pairs or groups, where a male ostrich is accompanied by several females and their immature young.

108 **Can you go without drinking water for several days?** Ostriches can do so as they use their metabolic water and suck out moisture from the roots, seeds and insects they eat. Of course, ostriches enjoy taking frequent baths and love water, wherever it is available. Did you know that ostriches have eyes that are about five centimetres across? This is the largest eye size of any land animal.

53

BIRDS AND REPTILES

109 **Ostriches can tolerate a very wide range of temperatures.** Can you believe, the temperature in the areas where ostriches live vary as much as 40 degree Celsius (100-degree Fahrenhite) between night and day. Their wings are specially designed to help them to deal with this temperature change.

110 **Rheas are also known as the South American ostriches.** There are only two species of rheas in the world today. The weight of this flightless bird is around 25 kilograms. Rheas have larger wings, but they cannot fly. They are generally brown in colour and are usually found near rivers or swamps.

111 **It is very strange but true that many people from New Guinea and even a boy from New Zealand have been killed by cassowary birds.** They are identified by a large bony crest on the forehead. The skin of their head and neck is very colourful, with markings of blue, purple and red. If someone approaches them, they are capable of attacking and kicking with their strong legs.

SPECIES, CHARACTERISTICS AND HABITAT

112 The emu bird is the second tallest bird in the world and is about 1.8 metres tall. It is very hard to distinguish between the sexes of this bird, but the female grows black feathers on her head and neck during the mating season. Their chicks have yellow and brown stripes along their sides and back.

113 Though penguins are birds, they are better adapted for an aquatic life. With the help of their narrow flippers which do not fold, penguins propel themselves through the water at the speed of around 19 km/hr. Penguin feathers are of uniform size and densely cover the entire body surface.

114 Did you know that the emperor penguin (Aptenodytes Forsteri) remains hungry for about two months, while it incubates its egg? During the bitter cold and darkness of the Antarctic winter, it breeds with its partner. When the female penguin lays its single egg, it is the male's responsibility to keep it warm. He tucks it under his belly skin on top of his feet until it hatches. During this period, he cannot move to find food.

BIRDS AND REPTILES

115 **The adelie penguins perform an interesting courtship display at their home in Antarctica.** The unmated males perform an 'ecstatic display'; they utter a drumbeat cry while stretching their head and neck upwards, and flap their flippers to and fro. Once they mate, they build a nest of stones, where the female penguin lays two eggs.

116 **As penguins don't have teeth, they use their beak to grab their prey.** They have a row of spines on the roof of their beak as well as spines on their tongue which help them get a good grip on their prey. They mainly find their food in the sea and mostly eat fish and squid. In one dive, a large penguin can collect up to 30 fish.

117 **Penguins lose about half of their body weight during the moulting period.** The moulting period is the time of the year when penguins lose their feathers. During this time, penguins are unable to go into the water, and spend their time on land or ice, till they grow new waterproof coats of feathers again.

SPECIES, CHARACTERISTICS AND HABITAT

118 **While hunting for food, penguins drink a lot of seawater.** They are able to do this because of the gland known as the supraorbital gland which is located just above their eyes. This gland filters the salt from their blood stream which is then excreted through the bill or by sneezing. To quench their thirst, penguins drink melted ice water from pools and streams.

119 **You will be amazed to know that penguins must oil themselves regularly.** Penguins produce a waterproofing oil through an adaptive gland also known as the preen gland. Penguins oil their feathers to insulate their bodies and reduce friction due to swimming. Penguins spend several hours on preening and caring for their feathers.

120 **Penguins are highly social birds and live in large colonies with their friends.** Some colonies contain populations of more than 20 million penguins. However, each penguin has a distinct call by which they can find their mates and chicks even in the largest groups. Penguins even swim and feed at sea in groups.

BIRDS AND REPTILES

121 Grebes are a widely distributed fresh water diving bird, and are grey and white in colour. They are poor fliers and awkward on land. When the parental horned grebes swim, their small chicks ride on their backs. These chicks even go underwater with their parents during dives, by riding between the wings on their parent's back.

122 Have you ever heard of a bird that can eat its own feathers? As the stomach of horned grebe usually contains a matted plug, they eat some of their own feathers. The function of the plug is to filter or hold fish bones till they can be digested. In order to start the plug of young grebes early, parents feed feathers to them.

123 Can you imagine a bird taking off like an aeroplane? Loons or divers, which are of the size of a duck, need a runway to take off! Loons run for a distance of about 30 yards up to a quarter mile (depending on the wind), across the surface of the water while flapping their wings, in order to gain sufficient speed for lift-off.

SPECIES, CHARACTERISTICS AND HABITAT

124 **Unlike other birds, loons have solid bones which makes it more difficult for them to float, but easier to dive.** To catch fish, loons stick their heads below water for a long time and then suddenly dive after their prey. Loons flatten their feathers to remove air from within their plumage and expel air from their lungs in order to swim quickly and dive deep.

125 **Have you wondered how long a bird can live?** Albatrosses can easily reach their 60th and even 70th birthdays, and even at that age they can lay eggs and raise their chicks. They are large, stout-bodied birds with long, narrow wings which make them excellent gliders. They also possess long tubular nostrils opening out from their hooked bills.

126 **Pelican birds breathe through their beaks as they don't have nostrils.** These birds also have four toes joined by skin to form a web. They are found in every continent except Antarctica. Pelicans prefer to live in warm regions and they feed on everything from fish and crustaceans to tadpoles and turtles.

BIRDS AND REPTILES

127 Pelicans catch their prey by swallowing them into the large gular sack (the featherless area of the throat) and then squeezing the water out from the side of their bill. They then move the food until the prey faces head-down in their throat, before swallowing it completely. Pelicans may even catch, drown and swallow a seagull, in case they are extremely hungry and desperate.

128 If you ever see flamingos, you will notice that their knees seem to bend backwards. In fact, this is not the case. Flamingos generally stand on their 'tip-toes', and the prominent visible joint of their leg is the ankle, while their knees are hidden by feathers. Thus, we usually mistake their ankles as their knees! Flamingos often stand on one leg with the other one tucked under their body.

129 Flamingos are filter feeders; they stir up the mud with their feet and then reach down to scoop up a beak full of mud and water. They spit out the muddy water, and sieve the food using tiny hair-like filters along the beak, called the lamellae. As they depend on shallow saltwater prey, they are usually found in mudflats or lagoons.

SPECIES, CHARACTERISTICS AND HABITAT

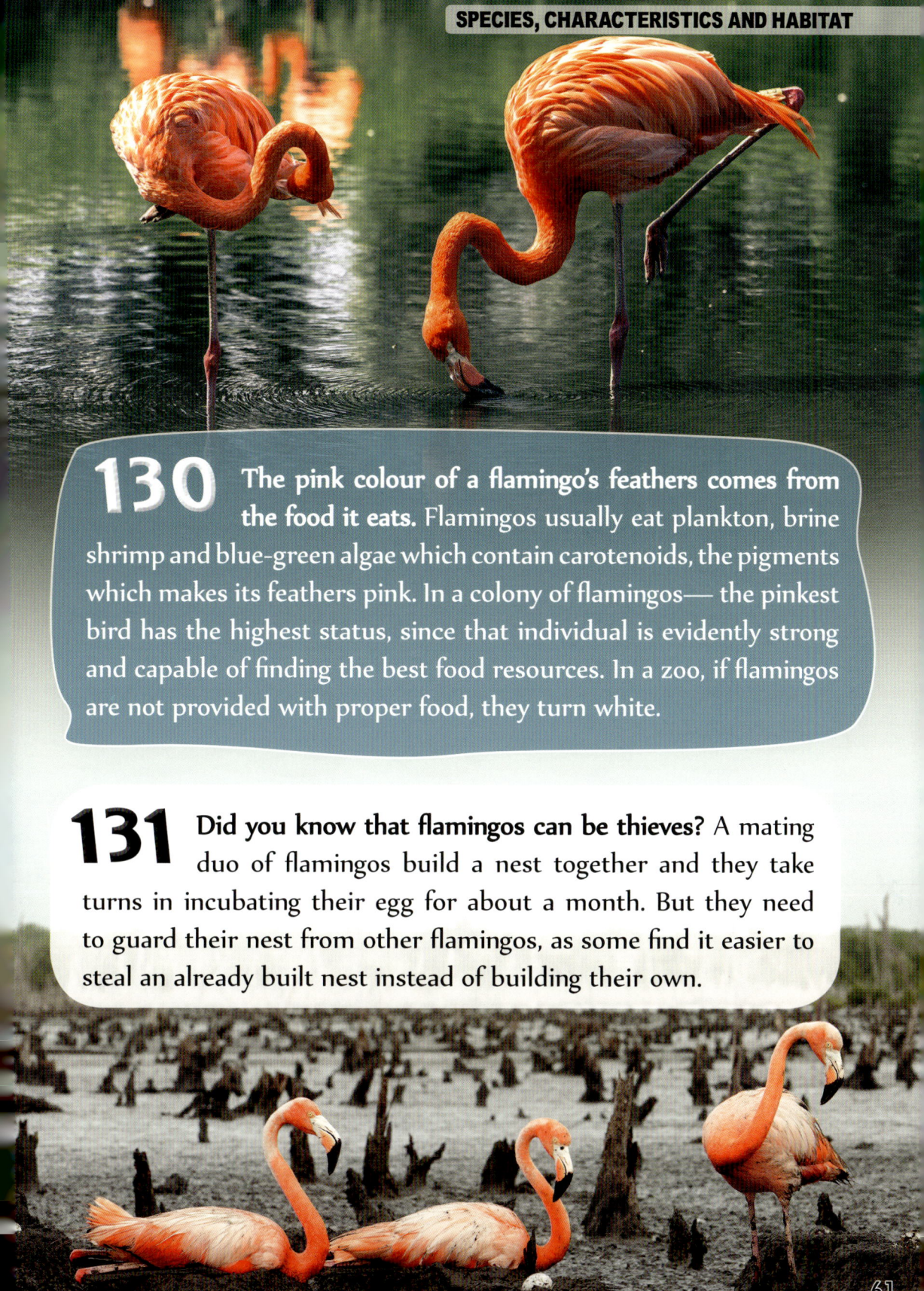

130 **The pink colour of a flamingo's feathers comes from the food it eats.** Flamingos usually eat plankton, brine shrimp and blue-green algae which contain carotenoids, the pigments which makes its feathers pink. In a colony of flamingos— the pinkest bird has the highest status, since that individual is evidently strong and capable of finding the best food resources. In a zoo, if flamingos are not provided with proper food, they turn white.

131 **Did you know that flamingos can be thieves?** A mating duo of flamingos build a nest together and they take turns in incubating their egg for about a month. But they need to guard their nest from other flamingos, as some find it easier to steal an already built nest instead of building their own.

BIRDS AND REPTILES

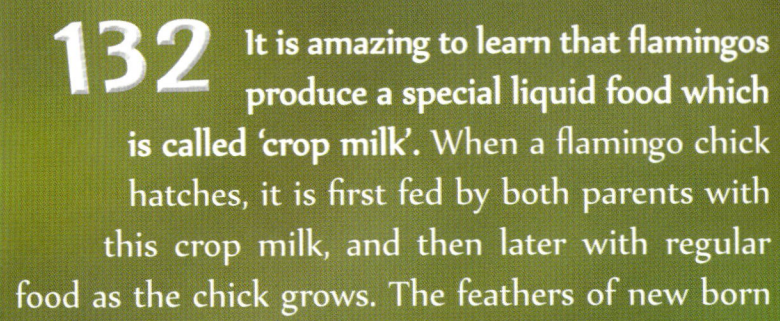

132 It is amazing to learn that flamingos produce a special liquid food which is called 'crop milk'. When a flamingo chick hatches, it is first fed by both parents with this crop milk, and then later with regular food as the chick grows. The feathers of new born chicks are usually grey and white, and it is only after about a year or so that they turn pink.

133 Heron birds are amazing flyers. They can fly at a speed of around 48 kilometres per hour. When they fly, their necks curl in an S-shape and legs swing behind their body, and they can quickly straighten their S-shaped necks towards their prey if they find any. Their main predators are minks, foxes and raccoons.

134 It is really hard to believe, but a heron bird can die of suffocation. If a heron tries to swallow a really big prey, it can choke and die. Herons generally hunt young birds and kill them, sometimes stealing eggs from their nest. Herons are active during both night and day, as they have specially designed eyes which help them to see equally well at night.

SPECIES, CHARACTERISTICS AND HAB

135 Herons generally build their nests on trees at least 25 metres above the ground in order to avoid stealing of eggs by predators. Nests are built using twigs, leaves and other plant material by both male and female herons. It takes a few days or few weeks to prepare a nest. But reed-bed herons build their nests on either cliffs, bushes or on buildings.

136 Have you ever wondered how ducks swim in icy water or walk on ice and snow? There are no blood vessels or nerves in the feet of ducks which means that they can't feel cold in their feet. Their feet are also webbed, and act like paddles under the water. This makes them good swimmers.

137 Swans have an amazing feature—they can sleep on either water or land. Swans can sleep while standing on one leg or while floating in the water. They are also believed to be highly intelligent, as they seem to be able to identify and recall the faces of people who have been kind to them. While swans are usually white, some swans are also found that are black in colour.

REPTILES

138 **Did you know that vultures have an acid in their stomachs which is almost comparable to battery acid?** This strong acid helps them to eat meat which could make any other creature sick. They can even consume remains that have rotted. They can even withstand the botulism bacterium to a strength of as much as a 100 times more than humans can.

139 **Have you noticed that the head and neck of vultures are bare?** As you know, vultures eat rotting carcasses which have a lot of bacteria and parasites that can cause infections to the birds' feathers. Thus, by not having any feathers in the neck area, the chances of such infections are nil among vultures.

140 **Did you know that ospreys are also called sea hawks? The birds hover over water to hunt fish.** As much as 99 per cent of the osprey's diet consist fish. The osprey's toes are reversible and they have sharp spicules on the underside of their toes. Most importantly, they have closable nostrils which help them keep water out during dives. Their talons also have backward facing scales, that act as barbs to hold the fishes they capture.

SPECIES, CHARACTERISTICS AND HABITAT

141 Like most birds, cranes too mostly communicate through loud sounds to their flock. Cranes have the ability to produce a wide variety of sounds. One such sound is the alarm sound which is produced to inform other cranes about an approaching threat.

142 Seagulls have proved to be very intelligent birds. They can learn, remember and even pass on behaviours. They stamp their feet in groups to imitate rainfall. As they can't eat hard shelled molluscs without opening them up, they simply drop molluscs onto rocks to crack open the shells. They also follow ploughs in fields to feed themselves from upturned grubs.

BIRDS AND REPTILES

143

Most creatures cannot **drink salt water.** However, though seagulls like to drink fresh water, they can also drink salt water. They have a special pair of glands right above their eyes, which flush the salt from their systems through openings in the bill, so that they don't get sick.

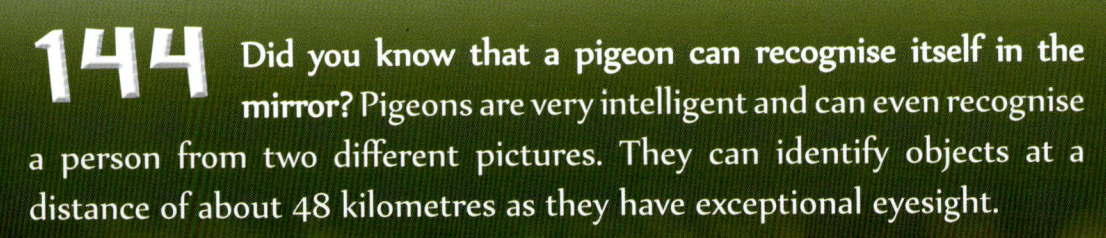

144
Did you know that a pigeon can recognise itself in the mirror? Pigeons are very intelligent and can even recognise a person from two different pictures. They can identify objects at a distance of about 48 kilometres as they have exceptional eyesight.

SPECIES, CHARACTERISTICS AND HABITAT

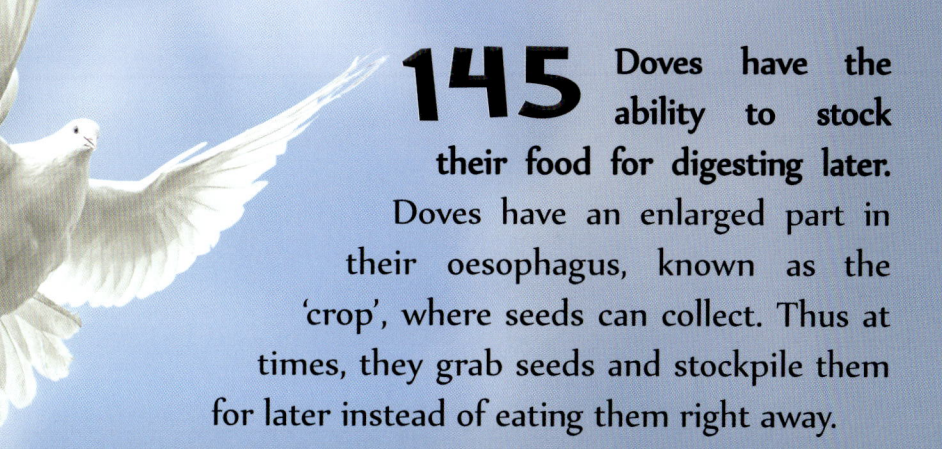

145 Doves have the ability to stock their food for digesting later. Doves have an enlarged part in their oesophagus, known as the 'crop', where seeds can collect. Thus at times, they grab seeds and stockpile them for later instead of eating them right away.

146 Keas are the only kind of alpine parrot in the world that can live in the cold environment high up in the mountains. Their bodies are rounded to preserve body heat and they have thick feathers to keep them warm. They are well-known for their curious behaviour, as they like to investigate bags, steal small items and peck at cars.

147 Do you know which bird lays the smallest egg? It is the hummingbird which lays the smallest egg—it is less than ½ inch long, but represents as much as 10 per cent of the mother's weight. The egg of hummingbird is smaller than a jelly bean!

BIRDS AND REPTILES

148 Wrens cannot bear cold weather as they have very small bodies and lose heat quickly. However, they do not migrate even in winter season, choosing to stay warm in their nests instead. If there is prolonged period of cold with sub-zero temperatures and snow covered ground, they can even die, as food is hard to find in such conditions.

149 Female yellow warbler use grass and bark to build their cup-shaped nests, and line them with deer hair, feathers, dandelions and cottonwood. They locate their nests usually 10 to 40 feet above the ground, in the trees. Yellow warbler nests are sometimes also used by brown-headed cowbirds to lay their eggs.

150 Starling birds gather in winter evenings and perform aerobatic display and murmurations before heading towards their sleeping site. By moving in flocks, the birds not only gain warmth from the sheer numbers, but also exchange information and provide safety to each other. This makes it difficult for predators to find an individual target in a large group.

SPECIES, CHARACTERISTICS AND HABITAT

151 About 300 million years ago in the Carboniferous Period, reptiles evolved from amphibians. With four legs and a tail, a reptile's skeleton has the same basic pattern as that of an amphibian. They have stronger teeth and their legs are also very strong and efficient which makes them more formidable hunters as compared to amphibians.

152 Reptiles are independent of water, but have also evolved waterproof skins. They keep moisture inside their bodies with the help of the scales that cover their body. Even the egg of a reptile has a protective and waterproof cover. Thus, aside from drinking water, they are completely independent of water, unlike amphibians.

153 Did you know that reptiles continue to grow in size until they die? Reptiles grow as long as food is available for them. Although the scales of reptiles do not grow, they moult frequently if food is available. In the moulting process, new skin is developed beneath, when the old skin becomes too tight, and then the old skin is shed.

BIRDS AND REPTILES

154 **Dinosaurs were reptiles.** Dinosaurs died out around 100 million years ago, but even today, they are the most famous reptiles. This group included the Diplodocus, Brontosaurus and Brachiosaurus, which were the largest animals which ever lived on land, at about 25 metres in length. On the other hand, some other dinosaurs were small and bird-like.

155 Scientists have found a species of crocodile—the phobosuchus hatchery—which was about 13.5 metres in length, and might have eaten large dinosaurs. On the other hand, another species, the theriosuchus, ate mouse-sized mammals and was less than 0.6 metres long.

156 Crocodiles often keep their mouths open as a way to regulate their body temperature. If a crocodile is out in the sun, it will become hot. It cannot sweat in order to cool itself, so it can either immerse itself in water, or lay on the river bank with its jaw wide open. By opening its jaw, the crocodile allows for the evaporation process through which it loses some of its heat, and cools down.

SPECIES, CHARACTERISTICS AND HABITAT

157 The crocodylus porosus (estuarine crocodile) is different from other crocodiles. Whereas most creatures in the crocodilian family are fresh water animals, this one is generally found along and in the mouths of rivers, where fresh water mixes with salt water. It is found in northern Australia and south-eastern Asia, as well as in the Solomon Islands and Fiji. It regularly swims between the islands of the Malay Archipelago.

158 By whirling round in the water and roaring, the male crocodile courts the female and then mates with her. Using mud or vegetation, or a mixture of both, some females make nests, while others dig a pit. They lay about 15 to 20 eggs in batches. The heat for hatching these eggs comes from the sun or the rotting vegetation around the nest.

159 Crocodiles usually preserve their prey for a while until it rots a little. This is because their teeth are not suitable for tearing up food. After the prey has rotted somewhat, the crocodile grabs the leg of the carcass, using its powerful jaws to break it down into pieces that can easily be swallowed. Inside the crocodile's stomach there are swallowed stones that help break up the food.

BIRDS AND REPTILES

160 Have you ever seen a gavial (gharial)? A harmless crocodilian with very long and slim snout, it is found mainly in the freshwaters of India. Gavial generally catch fish as its jaws are not very powerful. It sights its prey with its eyes positioned on the sides of the head and makes a swift sideways lunge with its jaws.

161 A female gavial always lays two layers of eggs. They build their nest in a unique manner—the female digs the nest and keeps about a foot of sand between the two eggs that she lays. As soon as the young hatch from their eggs, they are alert and start moving about rapidly.

SPECIES, CHARACTERISTICS AND HABITAT

162 **Turtles and tortoises are reptiles that are known as Chelonians.** Did you know that while their armour protects turtles, it also has a big disadvantage? Breathing is difficult for Chelonians as their ribs are attached to their shell. Thus, they cannot expand their ribs to draw air into their lungs. Movement of their head and limbs help Chelonians to pump air into their lungs instead.

163 **Turtles do not have teeth, but even then, they can deliver a nasty bite with their jaws.** Chelonian have very sharp and bony edges to their jaws which are covered by sharp horn. Using their sharp jaws, turtles are able to eat both animals and plants, despite not having any teeth.

BIRDS AND REPTILES

164 Terrapins are one of the species of turtle. When they are attacked, they have an additional defence mechanism. For instance, the musk turtle has a special type of gland on each side of the body. A very unpleasant fluid is produced in the glands which they discharge onto their attackers to defend themselves.

165 Some Terrapins wait for their prey to swim into their mouth, they don't chase it. The American alligator snapper (marcrochelys temmincki) sits at the bottom of a pond with its mouth open. It wriggles its pink, worm-like tongue, and fish often dive down in order to investigate this worm. As a result, they swim into the terrapin's mouth and get snapped up by it.

SPECIES, CHARACTERISTICS AND HABITAT

166 **Giant tortoises, in order to protect themselves from heat during the day, travel mostly at night.** They are only 1.5 metres in length and 0.75 metre in height and eat mainly cactus, leaves and berries, and hence are herbivorous. As many as 6,000 tortoises were imported from Rodriguez to Malaysia in the year 1759 by a ship.

167 **Lizards have been present on earth for around 180 million years and are older than their relatives, snakes.** There are many different kinds of lizards, such as land lizards, tree lizards, burrowing lizards, aquatic lizards and even aerial lizards. They vary in size from the over three-metre-long komodo dragon, to tiny geckos which are only a few centimetres long.

BIRDS AND REPTILES

168 Lizards are well-adapted to dry conditions and can easily live in deserts, but they cannot live in very cold conditions. Lizards also manage to live in the temperate zone, though a majority inhabit subtropical and tropical lands. In areas with extremely low temperatures, lizards have to hibernate as they cannot survive in very cold conditions.

169 **Lizards often have long tails.** The European green lizard has a tail that is 0.22 metres long, and the creature's complete length is 0.38 metres. This large lizard is distributed transversely across European mid-altitudes.

SPECIES, CHARACTERISTICS AND HABITAT

170 The male southern-Eurasia green lizard becomes brightly coloured and starts threatening other Lizards at the beginning of the breeding season. Though other lizards get frightened, the female green lizard does not. They mate and the female lays its eggs in a nest dug out of sand.

BIRDS AND REPTILES

171 Did you know that there is a lizard with a frill around its neck? The frilled lizard (chlamydosaurus kingii) raises a frill around its neck if frightened by a threat. They are large Lizards at around 0.85 metres in length, and spend most of their time in trees. They mainly eat insects and small vertebrates.

172 Flying Dragons, also called gliding lizards, contrary to their name, cannot fly. Instead, they use air currents to glide through air by using their wings. These wings are created by extending their connecting membrane and ribs. Thus, they are not capable of powerful flight but can glide as far as a distance of 60 metres. The total length of these flying lizards is usually only about 0.20 metres.

SPECIES, CHARACTERISTICS AND HABITAT

173 Marine iguanas can remain in water for an hour easily, but they usually stay underwater only for 15 to 20 minutes. They are of about 1.25 metres in length and greyish in colour. As they feed on seaweed growing on the rocks underwater, they dive down to a depth of about 4.5 metres for this purpose.

174 Lizards are amazing creatures that can fly, swim and even do acrobatics. Geckos are sometimes called the acrobats of the lizard world as they can run upside down across ceilings and can even travel across vertical glass. These small lizards are generally found in warmer lands across the world.

BIRDS AND REPTILES

175 **Have you wondered how geckos have this amazing climbing capability?** The toes of geckos are flattened and enlarged, and crossed by tiny flaps of skin called lamella. There are hundreds of tiny hooks in each lamella which provide them with a strong grip to climb any surface, even with irregularities.

176 **Geckos can shed their tail at will. This is a kind of defence mechanism.** A gecko can break its tail off by contracting a ring of muscle round its tail, if it is attacked. The fallen tail then makes twisting and squirming movements which attracts the attention of the attacker, while the gecko makes a getaway.

SPECIES, CHARACTERISTICS AND HABITAT

177 **You might have seen colour changing tree lizards in your gardens.** These are called chameleons. Unlike other lizards they are swivel-eyed, slow moving and grotesque to look at. They can easily move through twigs, as their toes are joined together to make curving hooks which clamp on opposite sides of a twig.

178 **A chameleon shows a strange combination of features.** They have a slow-moving body and a quick tongue. A chameleon tests each twig before putting its weigh on it, and moves very slowly through the branches of a tree or a plant. It can sight its prey within 1/25th of a second. It then shoots out its sticky tongue which hits the prey. The prey sticks to its tongue and is pulled back into the chameleon's mouth.

BIRDS AND REPTILES

179 **Chameleons are masters at changing colour.** They have two superposed thick layers of iridophore cells, which have a pigment that reflects light. There are nanocrystals of different sizes and shapes in these iridophore cells. By relaxing or exciting its skin, chameleons can change the structural arrangement of the upper cell layer which leads to change in colour.

180 **Did you know that out of about 3,000 species of lizards, only two can produce venom?** These are the gila monster and beaded lizard. Both the species have venom glands in their lower jaws, between their lips and gums. The poison accumulates in the grooves of their teeth, and thus these lizards hold their prey in their jaws and chew them to work sufficient poison into the wounds of the prey.

181 **The venom of the gila monster is a neurotoxin, which attacks the nervous system.** This poison is not very dangerous to man, and out of 34 cases of poisoning, only eight men died, who were either drunk or already unwell. However, even for a healthy human being, the venom can cause unpleasant effects like dizziness, swelling of glands and tongue, breathing difficulties and sickness. The bite area generally swells and is very painful.

SPECIES, CHARACTERISTICS AND HABITAT

182 Did you know that some lizards are leg-less? The worm lizards are completely legless. In fact, only experts can distinguish between worms and worm lizards, as they look very similar. These are burrowing lizards. The females of this family lay their eggs in ant's nests, so that the eggs get a suitable temperature and plentiful supply of ants to eat after hatching.

183 The glass lizard does not have limbs and looks very similar to a snake, hence it is also known as the glass snake. Like other Lizards, they too can shed their tail to distract predators, but the dropped part of the tail breaks into several pieces like glass. This is how they got their name. As they don't have limbs, they cannot tackle fast moving prey.

184 Snakes produce S-shaped curves as they move. Snakes don't have limbs and instead, glide along by means of their muscles and scales, and by lateral undulations of the body they produce S-shaped curves. It is believed that snakes evolved from burrowing lizards, as loss of limbs is certainly a feature of a burrowing life.

BIRDS AND REPTILES

185 Have you wondered how snakes catch prey if they don't have limbs? Snakes generally hunt their prey by sight, smell and sound; they tighten and squeeze their prey or kill them with poison. As snakes don't have external ears, they pick up sound vibrations along the length of their bodies. They can see well and even the flickering of their tongue helps locate the prey.

186 As snakes do not have limbs it is difficult for a male snake to hold onto the female during mating. Male snakes have evolved spined hemipenes, to ensure that the sperm enters the female body and fertilises her eggs. While most snakes lay eggs, some snakes, like rattlesnakes, hatch their eggs inside their body and give birth to live young.

187 There is some evidence that shows that snakes are reptilians, though they are not built on the typical reptilian pattern. There are still remains of back legs in some of the most primitive snakes. There are still present tiny claws at the base of their tails in certain blind snakes and boas.

SPECIES, CHARACTERISTICS AND HABITAT

188
Some snakes can fool their predators or attackers. One example of this is the Heterodon platyrhinos (American hog-nosed snake), which has a slightly distinct head from its neck. When attacked, this snake plays dead by turning on its back to confuse its predator.

189
There are some snakes that eat eggs. They swallow whole eggs which pass into a long projection that stretches from their backbone to their gullet. Here it is broken down, and the contents of the egg are passed on, while the shell is regurgitated and spit out. The dasypeltis species is an example of an egg-eating snake.

BIRDS AND REPTILES

190 **You will be amazed to know there are eight different types of venoms produced by different snakes.** They are: neurotoxin which attacks the nervous system, haemorrhaging which destroys blood vessel walls, thrombase which makes blood vessels clot, haemolysins which destroys red blood cells, cytolysins which destroy other cells, antifibrins which stop clotting, antibacterial which kills antibodies, and kinases which begin digestion.

191 Pit Viper is another name for the new world viper. These snakes have evolved a unique method of hunting. They have heat sensitive pits between the eyes and nostril on each side of their faces. The snake feeds on warm blooded animals which it hunts with the help of its pits.

SPECIES, CHARACTERISTICS AND HABITAT

192 **Sea snakes are elapid snakes with powerful poison.** Their bodies are well adapted to their aquatic life. As they swim through water, their flattened body moves from side to side, helping it pushing back in a S-shaped bend. The tail is flattened into a paddle shape which steers the snake. They are mainly found in the Indian and Pacific oceans and around Australia.

193 **To lay their eggs, a majority of sea snakes do not come ashore.** As these snakes are totally aquatic, they hatch their eggs inside their bodies and give birth to live young which can swim away as soon as they are born. The nostrils of these snakes have valves in them to prevent water from getting into their bodies.

194 **Reptiles are generally called 'cold blooded' animals, but that does not mean they have cold bloods in their bodies.** As reptiles are ectothermic, they get their body heat from external conditions. Humans have the capability to regulate body temperature, but these reptiles cannot maintain their body temperature, and are as warm or cold as the outside temperature.

BIRDS AND REPTILES

195 You will be amazed to know that there are snakes that can go months without eating. Snakes like the anaconda and the reticulated python, which are huge constrictors, belong to this group. These snakes have slower metabolism and they eat large meals relative to their body size. Thus, they can easily survive long gaps between meals.

196 Did you know that most snakes are not poisonous? Only around 30 to 40 species are considered harmful out of 500 snake species. But in Australia, poisonous snakes outnumber the non-poisonous ones. The inland taipan, found in Australia, is one of the most poisonous snakes in the world.

197 Do you know how many chambers there are in a reptile heart? Reptiles have three chambered hearts. Three chambered hearts are relatively inefficient in delivering oxygen to the body tissues, as it allows the mixing of oxygenated and de-oxygenated blood. Only crocodiles have four chambers in their heart, but when they are underwater they can shut off circulation to the lungs.

SPECIES, CHARACTERISTICS AND HABITAT

198 Reptiles perform excretion mainly through their kidneys. In diapsids like turtles, uric acid is the main nitrogenous waste. Reptiles don't have the loop of Henle in their kidneys, unlike birds and mammals, and hence are unable to produce more concentrated urine as compared to their body fluid. In some reptiles, excess salts are also excreted by nasal and lingual paths.

199 Do you know why snakes and lizards flick their tongue? They do so in order to capture the scent particles present in air. They hunt for their food by using their tongues to collect scent particles, which they send to Jacobson's organ to decipher, as they can't smell through their nose.

200 Due to its amazing ability to run over the surface of water, the basilisk lizard is also recognised as the Jesus Christ lizard. They travel over water with the help of fringes of skin on their rear feet and long toes. The tiny air pockets that they create by rapidly churning their legs protects them from falling into the water, provided they maintain their speed.

MAMMALS

Species, Characteristics and Habitat

201 **Mammals are warm-blooded animals.** This means that their body temperature remains constant. Mammals are found in all kind of terrains, climates and temperatures. We can find them living on land, water, sky and even under the ground. All mammals have hair and glands for producing milk. The largest mammal is the blue whale and the smallest is Kitti's hog-nosed bat.

202 **Mammals are divided into three groups— monotremes, marsupials and placental mammals.** Monotremes like the platypus, lay eggs. Among marsupials, like kangaroos, the young are not fully formed at birth. The mother carries the young in a pouch. The most common are the placental mammals. The young are nourished in the placenta before they are born. Humans are placental mammals.

203 **The platypus is one of the only four remaining monotreme mammals.** It means that they lay eggs instead of giving birth to their young. The male platypus has ankle spurs that are venomous. They also have a sense of electrolocation. This means that they can detect the electric field of their prey, using this to hunt.

SPECIES, CHARACTERISTICS AND HABITAT

204 **The kangaroo is the largest marsupial mammal.** The mother carries its young in a pouch till it is fully developed. Kangaroos have large feet and can jump up to 30 feet in a single bound! They have a strong tail that they use for balance while hopping. Kangaroos are social creatures and live in groups of 50 or more.

205 **Koalas are marsupial animals, carrying their young in the mother's pouch for seven months.** They have opposable thumbs, which allow them to grip branches, climb trees and hold their food easily. They are mostly nocturnal, sleeping for 18–20 hours a day! Koalas select a few trees as their 'home' and visit these regularly.

MAMMALS

206

Dolphins are one of the most intelligent animals. Their intelligence is displayed through their communication patterns. They have a signature whistle which helps others to identify them. They also teach their young to use tools. Dolphins use echolocation—using sound waves that bounce off objects nearby—to locate their prey.

207

Dolphins display signs of culture, something that was earlier considered a purely human trait. They are curious and playful in nature. They are often seen playing with each other as well as other species. They are also very social, living in groups called pods, hunting for food and raising their young together. They are also altruistic, often stopping to help others.

208

The gentle manatee loves to stay in water and is a good swimmer. Since it cannot breathe underwater, it surfaces frequently to breathe. The manatee can be found in shallow coastal regions and rivers. It is a herbivorous animal, munching on sea grass, spending almost half a day just eating. In fact, most of their body space is just taken up by stomach and intestines!

SPECIES, CHARACTERISTICS AND HABITAT

209 One of the most fascinating mammals is the whale. It may look like a fish, but in fact, it is a placental marine mammal. Although they spend their lifetime in the ocean, they do not have gills. Instead they must surface occasionally to breathe through their 'nostrils' or blowholes which are on their back.

210 There are many different species of whales. These are broadly divided into baleen whales and toothed whales. The blue whale is the largest animal to have ever lived on earth, larger than dinosaurs. The sperm whale can dive down to more than 2,000 metres. It also has the heaviest brain among animals, weighing close to nine kgs!

211 Many scientists believe that whales evolved from land animals. Examples of their marine adaptations include the blowholes that are modified nostrils, limbs that modified into flippers and layers of fat or blubber that allow these warm-bodied mammals to live in the cold oceans. Whales are very intelligent and quite noisy, often moaning, sighing and chatting with each other!

MAMMALS

212 **Seal are semi-aquatic marine mammals, living both in sea and on land.** They mostly live in the sea, coming ashore only occasionally. The whiskers of a seal are very important for them. They actually use these to hunt in the dark depths of the sea! The female seal is known as a 'cow' and comes ashore to give birth to her babies called pups.

213 **Unlike other sea mammals, sea otters rarely come ashore.** They also do not have a fat layer to protect themselves from cold water. Instead, they have water-resistant fur. Sea otters play an important role in maintaining the environmental balance of their habitat. They prey on undersea animals, preserving kelp forests that are vital for the marine environment.

214 **At 2.5 metres in length and an average weight of 680 kgs, the polar bear is the largest carnivore on Earth.** Despite its weight, it is also an excellent swimmer. It is found in extremely cold regions like the Arctic. Its thick fur and layer of blubber protects it from the cold. Did you know that under its white fur, the polar bear actually has black skin?

SPECIES, CHARACTERISTICS AND HABITAT

215 **Bats are the only mammals that can truly fly.** With over 1,000 species, bats account for a quarter of the mammal population on Earth! Bats are nocturnal creatures. They hunt in the dark by using echolocation. They make a high-pitched noise and then use the echo it creates to 'map' their surroundings.

216 **Native to North America, coyotes are incredibly adaptable.** They have adapted to new habitats, even human cities and towns. They are solitary creatures, but seek other's company during winters when they hunt in pack of two or three. They use different sounds to talk to each other—howling, yelping and barking. They are also great swimmers.

217 **The giraffe is the tallest mammal in the world.** A new-born is about six feet, taller than most adult humans! Giraffes need the shortest sleep among mammals, at just a little over two hours. These gentle creatures are social and rarely ever fight. You can identify different giraffes by their spot pattern. Like human fingerprints, these are unique to each giraffe!

218 There are over 30 species of foxes. They are solitary creatures, hunting alone. They often hide their food after a hunt and eat it later. They have acute hearing and can even hear noises from under the ground. The red fox is the most wide-spread carnivore in the world. The reason for its survival is its adaptability.

219 Wolves are social animals that live and hunt in packs. A wolf pack has a strict hierarchy with close bonds of affection and duty among its members. Pack members take care of their young and will even sacrifice their life for the pack. Wolves have a highly developed system of communication by which they communicate within a pack and with other packs.

220 Belonging to the mongoose family, the meerkat is a small, cat-like animal. They are found in African deserts and grasslands. Meerkats live in big groups known as a clan, mob or gang. They live in a complex system of underground tunnels that not only provide them protection from predators, but also offer them shelter during the day.

SPECIES, CHARACTERISTICS AND HABITAT

221 The aardvark is an unusual animal. Although it looks like a pig (in fact, the word 'aardvark' means 'earth pig' in South African), it is closer to the Elephant in its ancestry. Aardvarks have large front claws and a sticky tongue. They use their claws to dig and then slurp up their prey—termites and ants—with their sticky tongue!

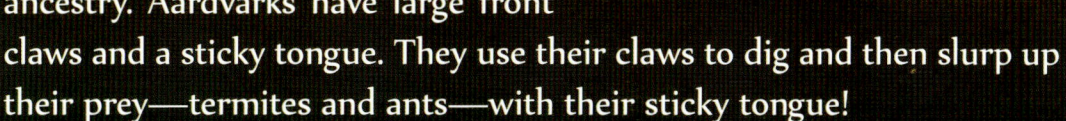

222 Giant pandas live in the bamboo forests in the mountains of central China. These black and white bears are omnivorous animals, but the bulk of their diet is bamboo. In fact, the pandas are big eaters. On an average, they eat for 12 hours and can consume almost 12 kgs of bamboo in a day! Unlike other bears, pandas do not hibernate.

223 **Chimpanzees are one of the great apes.** They are genetically very close to humans, sharing 98% of our DNA! They are omnivorous animals, eating a wide range of food. They live in communities with a rigid hierarchal structure. Although they walk on all fours, chimps can stand and walk upright. Native to Africa, they are an endangered species.

MAMMALS

224 Baboons are native to Africa and Arabia. The arms and legs of the baboon are almost the same length. Male baboons are twice as big as females. They are very social animals, living in large troops with a complex hierarchy. Their communication patterns also appear quite complex with different vocalisations, facial expressions, and gestures with hands and feet.

225 Gorillas are one of the great apes, sharing a close genetic make-up with humans. There are two species of gorilla—eastern and western which are further divided into sub-species. They are herbivorous. In fact, their roaming habits are critical in the dispersal of seeds around their habitat! Gorillas are ground-dwelling shy animals that live in groups.

226 Orangutan means 'person of the forest' in the Malay language. It is the only great Ape of Asia, native to the islands of Borneo and Sumatra. Orangutans are gentle and mostly solitary in nature. However, the females are constant companions to their immature young. They are the largest tree dwelling mammals. Orangutans also have an opposable thumb and an opposable big toe!

SPECIES, CHARACTERISTICS AND HABITAT

227 Native to the Amazon rainforests of South America is the pygmy marmoset. Weighing 100 grams, it is one of the smallest monkeys in the world. It can fit into an adult human's palm! Despite their small size, they can jump up to 15 feet and rotate their head to 180 degrees. They live in small troops of six or seven.

228 The grey langur is one of the most widespread monkey species found in the Indian subcontinent. They are also known as the Hanuman langurs after Hindu monkey god. They are found in a range of ecosystems—from mountain forests to deserts. The colour of their fur depends on their environment, since it doubles as a camouflage. They are herbivorous animals that live in small or big troops.

229 One of the best known species of deer is the reindeer. It is better known as caribou in North America. They are native to the polar region. Reindeers have several sub-species, some of which are endangered. When snow begins to fall, they migrate to warmer climates. In the process, the reindeers cover close to 1,600 miles in a year! Did you know that a reindeer's nose is adapted to warm the air before it breathes in?

MAMMALS

230 **Elk are large mammals, often counted in the deer family.** They have large antlers, measuring almost four feet. They shed these antlers in March, growing them back by May. Elks live in large herds, which are segregated by gender, forming a male herd and female herd. Elks migrate to cooler climes during summer, returning back during winters.

231 **Moose are the largest species in the deer family.** Males have distinctive large antlers, which measure about six feet end-to-end. The antlers drop off just before winters, but come back even bigger than before! Moose are herbivorous, solitary creatures. Males and females are of the same height, but the males are much heavier.

232 **The chital is an average-sized spotted deer.** It is found in the Indian subcontinent. Males are larger and have antlers that the females lack. A chital has a reddish-brown colour with white spots and a white underbelly. Females have a gestation period of 210 to 225 days, and they usually give birth every year.

SPECIES, CHARACTERISTICS AND HABITAT

233
Also known as the royal Bengal tiger, the white tiger is found in the Indian subcontinent, especially in the Sunderban forests in Bengal. They are the most common of the tiger sub-species. The white colour of some Bengal tigers comes from a mutated gene. No two tigers have the same stripes! Tigers are powerful, dominant predators and live a solitary life.

234
The beautiful snow leopard has a thick yellowish or light grey fur with black or brown rings. It has thick fur that covers its entire body, including the tail and paws. This is critical to survive in the cold conditions of its habitat in the mountains of Central Asia. They can jump as high as 50 feet.

235
The Jaguar has a yellow or orange coat and short legs. Jaguars are characterised by the dark spots on their coat. Shaped like small roses, these spots are called rosettes. Jaguars are commonly found in the American sub continent. They are big, powerful cats that live a solitary life. The Jaguar loves to play and hunt in water, unlike other big cats.

MAMMALS

236 The cheetah is the fastest land animal in the world, able to run as fast as 113 km/h. They can also turn mid-air while running. Cheetahs use their tails for steering when sprinting. The males are social and live in small groups, usually from the same family. The females, although solitary, are very affectionate and caring mothers.

237 Unlike the other big cats, the lion is a very social animal, staying in groups called prides. A pride has up to three males and a dozen or so females, usually related. The males have a thick mane that acts as protection when fighting. The male is responsible for maintaining a pride territory, while the females are the prime hunters.

238 The puma has the largest geographical range among mammals. Pumas are very adaptable and are found in a range of ecosystem. So wide is their natural habitat that over the years they have acquired over 80 names in different regions, which is more than any other animal in the world. Their many names include cougar, mountain lion, and catamount. Puma are solitary animals.

SPECIES, CHARACTERISTICS AND HABITAT

239 Although the black rhinoceros is herbivorous, it appears quite fierce. That's because it often charges with its horns pointed at the first hint of any danger! They have two horns which are made of a material similar to that of the human fingernail. Like the latter, it also continues to grow continuously. Females use their horn to protect their young.

240 After the elephant, the white rhino is the second largest mammal in the world. Both the white and black rhino are actually grey! Both have two horns, but their lip shapes differ. White rhinos are often seen playing around in the mud in water holes. The mud acts as a natural sun block and insect repellent!

241 Unlike its two-horned African cousins, the Indian rhino is one-horned. Unlike them, it also has a segmented hide which gives them better flexibility of movement. This allows them to easily change direction when running. Like other rhinos, it is also quite a nimble runner despite its size. It is often found near water, grazing on grass.

MAMMALS

242

The water-loving hippopotamus spends up to 16 hours in the water. Despite their huge size and weight (2,268 to 3,629 kg), hippos are graceful swimmers and can overtake a human while running on land! They produce a red oily secretion, which had created the myth of the hippo's bloody sweat. But the red substance is actually a natural moisturiser and insect-repellent!

243
Like the name suggests, a pygmy hippopotamus is the smaller cousin of the common Hippopotamus, and is **about a fifth of its weight.** Though they may look similar, there are other dissimilarities. Pygmy hippos have a narrower mouth, sleeker body and spend much less time in water. Unlike their bigger cousins, they prefer a solitary life.

244
Elephants are the largest mammal found on land. Elephants have massive bodies, big flapping years and a long trunk. They play critical roles in maintaining the ecosystem of their habitat. These herbivorous animals are peaceful and very intelligent. Their large body means that they need a lot of food to survive. So, they roam over vast distances looking for food.

SPECIES, CHARACTERISTICS AND HABITAT

245 An elephant's trunk is like a long nose, made of 100,000 muscles! It is used for breathing, grabbing things and lifting water. Elephants live in herds, which are often family units led by a matriarch. They are very intelligent animals with a good memory. Elephants are also empathetic creatures, showing grief and joy in their interactions.

246 There are two main elephant species—the African elephant and the Asian elephant. The African elephants are further divided into bush and forest elephants. The African elephant is slightly bigger with larger ears than its Asian counterpart. Unlike the African elephant, the Asian elephant plays a large role in local folklore and is used as a working animal.

247 Despite what its name suggests, the wolverine is actually the biggest member of the weasel family. They are found in arctic and subarctic regions. Wolverine is an omnivorous animal and also eats leftover dead meat. They are powerful solitary animals and usually roam over a large territory. Wolverines have a unique and individualistic pattern on their face, neck and chest.

MAMMALS

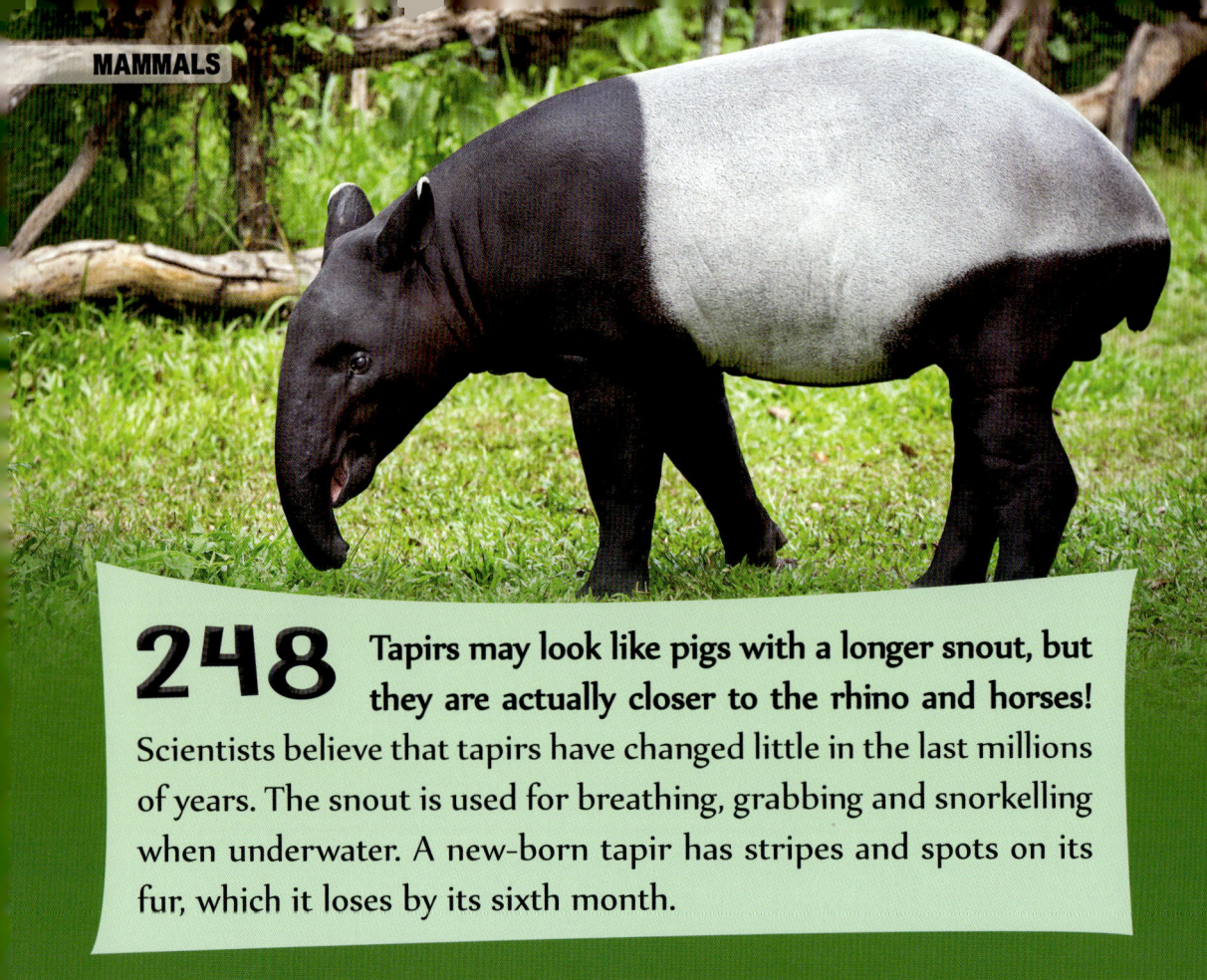

248 Tapirs may look like pigs with a longer snout, but they are actually closer to the rhino and horses! Scientists believe that tapirs have changed little in the last millions of years. The snout is used for breathing, grabbing and snorkelling when underwater. A new-born tapir has stripes and spots on its fur, which it loses by its sixth month.

249 The African wild dog is highly social, living in packs that is led by a dominant pair. They are wanderers and each pack has a large territory. They are intelligent animals that hunt as a pack. They are also cooperative and peaceful when feeding, rarely fighting over the spoils of their hunt and feeding their pups first.

250 Native to the island of Madagascar, the fossa is related to the mongoose. Growing up to six feet, it is the largest carnivore on the planet. It is also the island's top predator. This solitary animal is fast and agile. Its tail is used for balance when it jumps or hangs from treetops.

SPECIES, CHARACTERISTICS AND HABITAT

251 **The barrel-shaped giant armadillo's body is completely covered in a hard shell that acts as armour.** Their forefeet have formidable claws. They are very agile, using their tail for balance. The three-legged armadillo curls into a ball when it faces a threat. Did you know that a female armadillo can actually 'postpone' her pregnancy till suitable conditions appear?

252 **Native to Australia, the numbat is a rare marsupial mammal that does not have a pouch.** Instead, long hair on the belly cradle the new-born for five months, after which the young stays in a nest while the mother forages for food. This small solitary mammal feeds on termites, ants and insects.

253 **Pangolins are the only animals covered in scales.** Their scales are made of keratin—a hard substance that also makes our nails. Pangolins are insectivorous. They use their long sticky tongue to 'slurp' up insects. In fact, their tongue, when fully extended, is longer than the pangolin's head and body! Did you know that the Pangolin does not have teeth? Instead, it swallows stones and uses them to grind food in the stomach!

MAMMALS

254

Like it name suggests, the Tasmanian devil is a bad-tempered animal found in Tasmania, Australia. It is a marsupial mammal. Females give birth to up to 50 offspring, who have to race to the mother's pouch for nourishment. Despite their small size, they are ferocious in their temper.

255 **The powerful and formidable brown bear is found all over the world.** This omnivorous animal is known for its habit of going into hibernation over the long winter months. During autumn, it eats around the clock. As winter approaches, the now fattened bear goes to a pre-selected cave to sleep. Females do not even wake up to give birth!

256 **Native to North America, the black bear is smaller than the polar bear and white bear.** They are excellent climbers, with the cubs often climbing trees for fun and protection. They are also great swimmers. black bears have a shuffling walk, but can run quite fast. However, because of their bulky bodies, they cannot keep up the pace for a long time.

SPECIES, CHARACTERISTICS AND HABITAT

257 Also known as the Andean bear because of its home in the Andean mountains, the spectacled bear is the only bear species found in South America. They get their name from the distinctive markings on their face. They are agile climbers who prefer to spend their time on trees, building platforms with branches to rest.

258 The forelegs of the brown hyena are longer than its hind legs, giving its body its characteristic sloping appearance. They have a brown-coloured shaggy coat and a short tail. They live in clans with a strict hierarchy. Although they share their spoils with the clan, they do not hunt in a pack. They also often hoard surplus food and eat it later.

259 The Narwhal has a long tusk on its face, earning it the title of 'unicorn of the sea'. The tusk is actually a tooth that grows through the male narwhal's upper lip. It can grow up to nine feet! Females rarely have this tusk. They swim in groups, known as pods. These rare sea mammals are usually found in the Arctic region.

MAMMALS

260 The sea lion looks like a seal and is also a semi-aquatic animal. But there are many points of dissimilarity with seals. For instance, the sea lion has external ear flaps and walks on all four flippers when on land. It is a social animal, living and travelling in a group. Sea lions are highly intelligent, with some species like the Galapagos sea lion showing lively curiosity.

261 Native to the Indian subcontinent, the sloth bear has shaggy, messy looking fur. They are omnivorous, eating insects and fresh fruit. They also climb trees to bring down honeycombs, from which they feed. Unlike other bears, the sloth bear does not hibernate—since it lives in hot jungles, it does not need to hibernate.

262 The busy beaver is a rather clever mammal. Like humans it can engineer its environment to suit its needs. Beavers build dams, lodges and canals which can be used for protection as well as shelter. They are also great swimmers. They can even stay underwater for 15 mins. Beavers live in large family groups with monogamous parents and other siblings.

SPECIES, CHARACTERISTICS AND HABITAT

263 It may look like a buffalo, but the American bison is actually closer to cows and goats. Despite its weight (up to 1,000 kgs), it is surprisingly agile. It can race to 40 mph, jump as high as six feet and quickly turn around when pursued by predators. Bisons in America are also raised as livestock.

264 **The water buffalo is found in muddy waters and tropical swamps of Asia.** It has big hooves that prevent it from sinking into the soft muddy ground. It spends most of its time in water because of the high temperatures in its habitat. The males have a crescent-shaped horn that can grow as long as five feet.

265 **Yaks live in extreme cold temperatures of less than -40 degrees Celsius.** Their long, shaggy outer coat has an inner layer of shorter fur, giving them insulation against cold. Their dense horns also help in digging through the snow. They have split hooves, which help them to move nimbly on icy terrain. Yaks also huddle together for extra warmth.

MAMMALS

266 The African buffalo is the only wild cattle species found in Africa. It is a large animal with massive horns that resemble a question mark. They are usually found in large herds with numbers up to a 1,000. They have an excellent memory and remember their hunters, from humans to lions.

267 Zebra stripes are unique to each animal. They are also powerful camouflage. When they come together in a herd, the stripes can confuse predators. Zebras are highly social and often live in big herds known as harems. They are very caring and will come back to help an injured group member when under attack.

268 There are 25 different species of the chipmunk, 24 of which are native to North America. Chipmunks are solitary creatures who live in underground burrows. They spend most of their time foraging for food. They have cheek pouches that enable them to carry a lot of food to their burrows. Chipmunks go into hibernation during winters.

SPECIES, CHARACTERISTICS AND HABITAT

269 Known for hibernating in winter, the groundhog is a large squirrel that lives on the ground. The groundhog spends much of its time eating and building fat reserves on its body. It builds burrows just beneath the surface of the ground, which can extend up to 66 feet. The burrows act as shelters when winter sets in.

270 The hedgehog has as many as 5,000 spines that cover its entire body except its face, legs and belly. Each spine will last a year after which it will drop and a replacement will grow back. When faced with a predator, the hedgehog curls into a ball to protect its stomach. These solitary creatures go into hibernation in extreme cold or hot conditions.

271 The jackrabbit is not actually a rabbit. It is a hare. Jackrabbits are nocturnal, solitary creatures. They are larger than rabbits, have fur, long ears and longer hind legs. Their powerful hind legs enable them to jump up to 10 feet. They are also fast and agile, running in a zigzag pattern when escaping from a predator.

MAMMALS

272 **The porcupine's body is covered with long, sharp quills.** Some porcupines have as many as 30,000 quills! Usually the quills will lie flat, but stand up when the porcupine is under attack. The quills are a defence mechanism. They detach when touched and are very difficult to remove. Porcupines are good climbers and spend most of their time on trees.

273 **Raccoons are characterised by the distinct colouration of their body.** They have a black band around their eyes that resembles a mask, as well as black and brown bands on their tails. A racoon's front paw resembles a human's and is almost equally dexterous. Raccoons are known for their adaptability with a wide range in diet and habitats. Did you know that raccoons are very finicky about cleanliness? They are known to wash their food in streams before eating it!

274 **You can smell a skunk before you see it!** These small furry animals can release an extremely foul odour, which is very hard to get rid of, as a defence mechanism against predators. The smell comes from glands that rest just under its tail. When threatened, the skunk turns around and releases this horrible scent!

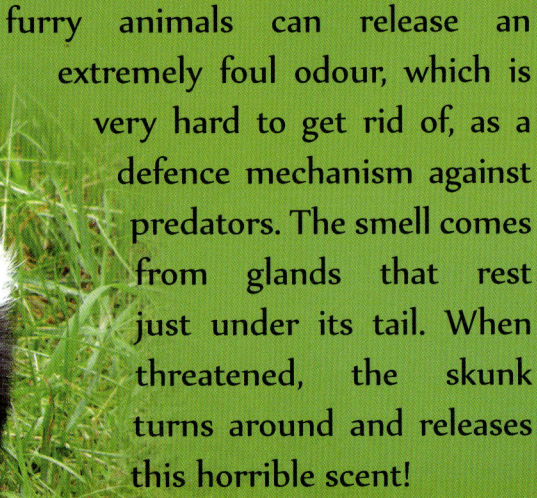

SPECIES, CHARACTERISTICS AND HABITAT

275 Known for its eerie laugh, the spotted hyena is the second largest carnivore in Africa. Although they have a notorious reputation as scavengers in the wild, in reality the hyenas are formidable hunters. They are complex, social creatures that follow a matriarchal set up in its clan, a rarity among mammals.

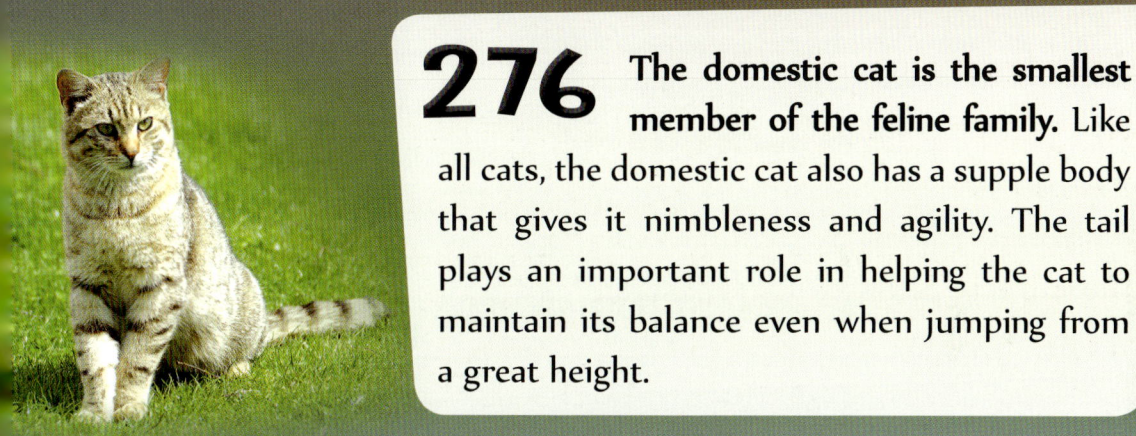

276 The domestic cat is the smallest member of the feline family. Like all cats, the domestic cat also has a supple body that gives it nimbleness and agility. The tail plays an important role in helping the cat to maintain its balance even when jumping from a great height.

277 Cows are social and emotional animals like humans. Like us they are close to few individuals and may take a dislike to others. They also feel emotions like excitement, affection, happiness, anxiety and curiosity. Their stomach is divided into four compartments that help in efficient digestion. Cows also have a 360° vision that helps them in spotting any threat.

MAMMALS

278 The warthog may look ferocious, but it is quite a peaceful animal. The animal gets its ferocious appearance from the two pairs of tusks on its face. The upper tusks are sharp and curved. Interestingly, the warthog is able to survive in areas with little water, as it can manage for long periods without it.

279 The bactrian camel has two humps and is found in the rocky deserts of East Asia. A number of evolutionary features have helped them to survive in harsh desert conditions. Their humps store fat, which is then converted to energy and water when required. They have a protective shaggy coat in winters. They also have bushy eyebrows and two rows of long eyelashes to shield from desert sun.

280 The Arabian camel may have just one hump, but it can store up to 36 kilograms of fat. It can break down the fat for sustenance when needed. Its flat, padded feet help it to cover vast distances, up to 161 kilometres, in the desert. This makes the camel an essential pet for people living in and around deserts.

SPECIES, CHARACTERISTICS AND HABITAT

281 It may not seem so, but pigs are one of the most intelligent mammals after humans. They are curious, sharp and their many 'oinks' and grunts show a developed communication ability. They are social animals who love to stay with their own kind. Despite their reputation of being very dirty, they are actually very clean, even separating their toilet areas from living areas!

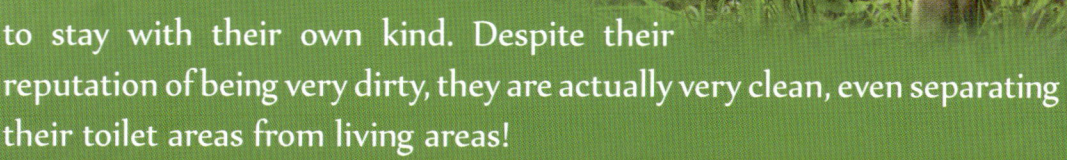

282 The wild boar is the wild forefather of the domestic pig. It is one of the most widespread mammals in the world. Unlike the domesticated pig, it has a double coat of fair with an outer layer of bristly hair and softer undercoat. It also has long, curved tusks on its bottom lip. Boars are social and live in female-dominated groups called 'sounders'.

283 The guinea pig is neither a pig, nor does it come from Guinea! Once a wild rodent species, it was domesticated by the Incas. Guinea pigs need to eat foods that give them vitamin C, since they cannot make it in their bodies. Like other rodents, the guinea pig's teeth are constantly growing. They keep chewing and gnawing on food which wears down their teeth.

MAMMALS

284 **Native to South America, the alpacas are a domesticated species related to camels.** It is the smallest member of the camel family. They are bred for their fine, dense and soft fleece. They are social animals and are usually bred in a herd. Alpacas are known for their habit of spitting. They spit when upset or threatened, or to establish dominance.

285 **Closely related to and resembling the alpacas, the llama is also completely domesticated.** They are bred as pack animals. They can survive on many different kinds of plants and very little water, making them ideal for long treks in harsh mountainous conditions. Llamas can be stubborn. An over-laden llama will hiss, spit and refuse to move!

286 **The guanaco is a wild camelid species found in South America.** In fact, it was once believed that they were the wild ancestors of the domesticated llamas and alpacas. Like camels, guanaco have thick eyelashes to protect their eyes against the wind and dirt of their mountainous habitat. Like alpacas and llamas, the guanaco also resort to spitting when upset!

SPECIES, CHARACTERISTICS AND HABITAT

287 Goats were among the first animals that were domesticated. They are intelligent and inquisitive with deep interpersonal bonds. Mothers and kids can identify each other's bleats when separated and always stay close by. They are very agile. Some breeds can climb trees and trek over mountainous terrain.

288 Contrary to their reputation as dumb herd animals, Sheep are some of the most intelligent mammals. They have very good memory and communicate through bleats and facial expressions. They will even self-medicate, eating only plants that would cure them. A sheep named Dolly was the first mammal that was cloned!

289 Known for their large, curving horns, bighorn sheep are found in the mountains of North America. At 14 kgs, their horns are very heavy. In fact, the weight of a bighorn sheep's horns is more than all its bones combined! They have special hooves that help them maintain balance on rocky terrain. The bighorn are social, but prefer the company of their own gender with separate male and female herds.

MAMMALS

290 The opossum or possum is a clever little animal. When faced with a predator it will flop on the ground, stare at the sky and hang out its tongue, pretending that it's dead! This behaviour gave rise to the phrase 'playing possum'. It is a marsupial mammal. Newborn Possums, as tiny as honeybees, crawl into the mother's pouch where they develop further.

291 Known as 'man's best friend', dogs are believed to be the first animals that were domesticated. They are very intelligent with a very strong sense of smell. Dogs also have a sense of time. They can sense and share our emotions. They will even miss you if you are gone for a long time. One study claims that dogs can sense the Earth's magnetic field!

292 Horses are known for their intelligence and grace. Domesticated for transportation, horses are fast and muscular enough to carry both cargo and humans. They are social animals who like to live in herds. Horses can sleep both standing up and lying down. They also have a near 360° visions, except for blind spots directly in front and at the back.

SPECIES, CHARACTERISTICS AND HABITAT

293

Przewalski's horse or the Dzungarian horse is found in Mongolia. It is the only remaining breed of wild horses in the world today. They were near extinction, but were successfully reintroduced in the wild. Shorter than most domesticated horses, they are social and affectionate animals. There are also some feral horses that escaped domestication, adapting to the wild, such as mustangs and brumbies.

294

The sloth can easily win the prize for the laziest mammal. They spend most of the day sleeping in trees. So slow is their movement that algae can actually grow on their fur! Their slow movement and the green algae on their bodies also work as excellent camouflage. Sloths have long claws that help them hang on to tree branches for eating and sleeping. They are usually found in the tropical climates of Central and South America.

295

The gerbil is a small rodent that lives in burrows. There are over 100 different species of gerbils, and the colour of their fur depends on their species. They have long hind legs that aids in jumping. A gerbil will thump its leg on the ground as a warning when confronted with a threat. They are territorial animals with an acute sense of hearing.

MAMMALS

296 Found in Australia and nearby islands, wombats are marsupial animals. The newborn will stay in its mother's pouch for roughly five months. Even after emerging, the young will hide back into its mother's pouch when threatened. They are burrowing animals, creating burrows with chambers. Some species are solitary, while some are social.

297 The 13 lined ground squirrel is called that because of the thirteen brown and white stripes on its body. They have sharp eyesight and often stand on their hind legs to observe their surroundings. They build burrows as long as 200 feet long! Unlike animal packs, this squirrel's pack lacks any particular structure.

298 The ring-tailed coati is found in the tropical forests and forests of South America. It gets its name from the black rings appearing on its tail. They are omnivorous and forage for food on both the ground and treetops. Females live in groups of 15 to 30 coatis, known as brands, while the males live solitary lives.

SPECIES, CHARACTERISTICS AND HABITAT

299 The chinchilla looks like a cute rabbit, but is more closely related to porcupines and guinea pigs. They have thick fur that protects them in the high altitudes of the Andes, where they are found. The chinchillas almost became extinct because of high demand for their fur, which was used for clothing. They are very social and live in colonies in burrows. Female are dominant among the chinchillas.

300 Capybara are the largest rodents, and are found in Central and South America. They like water and are seen near water holes like swamps and rivers. Like cows, they regurgitate their food and chew the cud. Capybaras were near extinction a few years ago, due to excessive hunting. Successful conservation methods have brought back their numbers.

INSECTS AND CRUSTACEANS

Species, Characteristics and Habitat

301 **Studies have shown that insects make up about three-quarters of all animal species on Earth.** These insects play a very important role in keeping the ecosystem healthy. They break down organic matter to enrich our soil and provide food for larger animals.

302 **The Hercules beetle is found in the rainforests of Central America, South America, Lesser Antilles, and the Andes.** Some of them can grow to more than 15 centimetres in size. These beetles are really strong and can lift 850 times their own weight. In human terms, it is equal to a man lifting 10 elephants!

303 **Honeybees produce honey and construct perennial nests from wax.** The honey that they produce is very useful for human beings. It is believed that a single bee makes about 10 million trips to collect enough nectar to produce the amount of honey that could fill a 450 gram jar.

304 **Over 200 ant species are known as army ants or legionary ants in different lineages.** These species form aggressive predatory foraging groups called 'raids'. Army ants do not build permanent nests like the other species of Ants; rather, the colony keeps moving from one place to another over time.

SPECIES, CHARACTERISTICS AND HABITAT

305 **Army ants travel in huge numbers.** Often hundreds and thousands of them travel together while attacking any animals that come in their path. The small workers among them sting the prey, while the larger soldier ants have big jaws and defend the troop against any threat.

306 **Most crustaceans live in the ocean, but some of them also live in fresh water and some live on land.** Some of them even live attached to rocks or sides of ships. Crabs, prawns, shrimps, lobsters and barnacles are all classified as crustaceans.

307 **Different crustacean eat different kinds of foods.** Some of them are scavengers that live on scraps or dead creatures. Some of them, like crabs, shrimps and prawns, search for food at night and hide inside the cracks of rocks by the day. Some are also herbivorous, that eat plant remains.

INSECTS AND CRUSTACEANS

308 Studies have shown that there are around 44,000 different species of crustaceans around the world. All the crustaceans have an exoskeleton which they have to shed in order to grow because the exoskeleton does not grow. This hard exoskeleton protects their body. They do not have a skeleton inside their body.

309 One of the two largest spiders in the United Kingdom is the raft spider or the Jesus spider. It has the ability to walk on water and hunts by running across the surface of water. It can also completely submerge itself inside water to hide from predators. It can stay submerged for as long as one hour under the water by using air bubbles trapped under the hair on its body.

310 There are small, pinkish, shrimp-like creatures in the ocean that are called krill. They are small crustaceans found in all the oceans of the world. They usually are found together in huge numbers and are the main diet of many larger sea creatures. They are a vital part of the marine food chain.

SPECIES, CHARACTERISTICS AND HABITAT

311 The golden orb-web spider spins very large webs and is known for spinning impressive webs that could be as large as one to two metres across. It is also believed to make the strongest silk. These spiders are also known as golden orb-weavers or giant wood spiders. Their webs are strong and wide and are built to catch wasps, flies, and can even catch butterflies.

312 The silk produced by the golden orb-web spider has many useful qualities. Several efforts have been made in the past to produce garments from this silk but none of them seemed feasible for commercial use. The silk produced by 1.2 million spiders were made into a shawl that was exhibited in 2009 at the American Museum of Natural History.

313 The huge webs made by the golden orb-web spiders are very helpful for some fishermen. The fishermen that work on the coasts of the Indo-Pacific Ocean take this web and ball it up, before throwing it into the water, where it unfolds and is useful for catching bait fish.

INSECTS AND CRUSTACEANS

314 **Ladybirds are one of the most beautiful insects we can see in our garden.** They are usually red in colour with black dots on their wings. They are called ladybugs in the United States and lady beetles in Europe. They feed on aphids and are known to be a gardener's friend for killing off pests from the garden, agricultural fields and orchards.

315 **All ladybirds do not have spots; some of them even have stripes.** Most of the ladybirds are red, orange, or yellow in colour with black spots. However, several ladybirds are entirely grey, brown or black in colour.

316 **There is a group of beetles known as tiger beetles.** They are one of the fastest among all insects. These beetles are well-known for their running speed and their aggressive predatory habits. There are around 2,600 known species and sub-species of these beetles, of which the richest diversity is found in the oriental region.

SPECIES, CHARACTERISTICS AND HABITAT

317 **Tiger beetles are known for their great speed.** One of its species is the Australian Tiger Beetle that can run at a speed of nine kilometres per hour when chasing its prey. This is a very impressive record for such a small insect.

318 **Midges include some very small winged flies which are commonly found in almost every country.** Midges are not termed as any one particular group, but various small species come under it including the black fly, sand fly, and others. Many midges spread diseases to humans as well as animals.

319 **Some species of midges beat their wings at an astonishing speed.** It is said that some of them can beat their wings to the tune of 1,000 beats per second. This is faster than any other creature. There are also some non-biting midges that can be found around man-made water bodies, which are mistaken for mosquitoes.

320 Lobsters belong to a family of large marine crustaceans. They have five pairs of legs out of which three pairs have claws. The first pair of legs is usually much larger than the rest. They have muscular tails. Lobsters live in the crevices on the floor of the sea.

321 Lobsters are among the famous seafood in the world. Lobsters can be of various colours. There are yellow, orange, blue, and white coloured Lobsters. But there are no red coloured lobsters. A lobster only turns red when it is cooked.

322 Crustaceans vary in sizes, from very small ones to very large ones in the sea. The smallest of the crustacean is the stygotantulus stocki, which measures only 0.004 inches in length. Its name commemorates a Dutch carcinologist, Jan Hendrik Stock.

SPECIES, CHARACTERISTICS AND HABITAT

323 One of the species of the marine crab is the Japanese spider crab. It is believed to be the largest crustacean in the world. It has the largest leg span of all the crustaceans, reaching up to 18 feet from claw to claw.

324 The Japanese spider crab is said to have a gentle nature despite a fearsome appearance. It is orange with white spots along its legs and also uses camouflage to protect itself from predators. The Japanese name for the crab is 'taka-ashi-gani' which means 'tall legs crab'.

325 Many crustaceans are used as sea food all over the world. One of the delicacies is the soft shell crab. These soft shell crabs are basically crabs that have moulted out of their exoskeleton in order to grow and their new shells are not hardened yet.

INSECTS AND CRUSTACEANS

326 **Crickets are insects that have cylindrical bodies with round heads and long antennae.** They also have wings that are folded when not in use for flight. However, many species of crickets are also flightless. Bull crickets are the largest members of the family and can measure up to two inches long.

327 **Crickets are known for their chirping.** Most male crickets make chirping sounds by stridulation, which means by rubbing parts of their body. Most females of the species lack the necessary body structure for stridulation, and hence they do not make any sound.

328 **Many insects have their body parts placed in a different way than human beings.** As mammals, we have ears at the side of our head, but crickets have ears on their front legs. There are some hawk moths that have ears on their mouthparts. Also, mantidae have ears between their back legs.

SPECIES, CHARACTERISTICS AND HABITAT

329 **Grasshoppers are also known as locusts.** Like crickets, they also make sounds by stridulating. Although grasshoppers have powerful legs that help them to jump, they also have wings that help them to fly away from their predators. Most of the time, their jump gives them a boost into the air, to help them fly.

330 **The legs of lobsters have chemosensory hair on them that are used to identify food.** There are small antennae in front of their eyes that are used for tracking food that is farther away. They have a set of teeth inside their stomachs which they use to chew food inside it, which is called the gastric mill.

331 **Lobsters can regenerate limbs that are cut off from their bodies.** This happens at a much slower rate as compared to other animals that can regenerate their body parts. For instance, if a claw is cut off from a one-pound lobster, it will take the creature almost five years to regenerate a claw of the same size.

INSECTS AND CRUSTACEANS

332 When lobsters are put into the hot pan while cooking, they do not scream. The main reason for this is because they cannot process pain, and also because they do not have vocal chords. The noise that is heard while cooking them is the sound of the air trapped in their stomach which is forced out through the mouth.

333 The Coleoptera order of insects consists various kinds of beetles. There are more than 380,000 species in this order. According to a recent study, the reason behind the beetle diversity in this order is because of their versatility in lifestyle. This also ensures that the species do not easily go extinct like other mammals or amphibians.

334 Coleopteran beetles have evolved in a variety of shapes and colours. They can range from around 0.4 millimetres to 80 millimetres in length. Australia alone has around 117 families of beetles, ranging over some 28,000 species of the insect. Beetles have two pairs of wings with the forewings being harder than the hindwings.

SPECIES, CHARACTERISTICS AND HABITAT

335 **Beetles can be found in almost every kind of environment.** Most of the beetle families are terrestrial, but many have habitats in freshwater or live in marginal marine environments. They can be found anywhere including under the bark of living or dead trees, in dung, in muddy flats, and in humus or leaf litter.

336 **Ants are the most common kind of insects that we see on our planet.** We can see them outside or even inside our homes. In a scientific research, it was found that around 10 quadrillion ants live on Earth at any given moment. When we compare them with human beings, we can easily say that there are 1.4 million ants per human being if the world population is of 7.3 billion people.

337 **Apart from Antarctica, insects can be found in huge numbers everywhere on this planet.** Only one species of insects can be found on Antarctica—Belgica antarctica, a wingless midge around 0.2 to 0.58 centimetres long. It can prevent its bodily fluids from freezing in the cold. It is dark purple-black in colour, allowing it to absorb as much visible sunlight and heat as possible.

INSECTS AND CRUSTACEANS

338 All crustaceans are different from one another when it comes to method of swimming and travelling. While crabs and shrimps can swim, lobsters only scuttle about at the bottom of the ocean. Barnacles are another kind of crustacean that stick themselves to some hard surfaces like rocks or boats and never move.

339 Crabs have their own shells—the exoskeletons that are moulted by the crabs in order to grow. But there is one kind of crab that does not make its own shells. Hermit crabs hide in the shells that are left behind by other animals because they do not make shells for themselves.

340 Shrimps walk slowly when they move across the sea floor. While fleeing from a predator shrimps swim backwards by curling and uncurling their abdomen. This reaction is known as the caridoid escape reaction. This reaction is also called 'lobstering' or 'tail-flipping'.

SPECIES, CHARACTERISTICS AND HABITAT

341 Fiddler crabs are also known as calling crabs. Female crabs have both their front claws of the same size, while male crabs have one of their claws bigger than the other. The males used this claw to impress females by waving it in the air. They also use their bigger claw to intimidate other male crabs and predators.

342 The arrow crab is also known as the spider crab because of its appearance. It has a unique pointed head and extremely large legs. It is named 'arrow' because of the angular features of its body. Females are smaller than the males of the species, but they can grow up to 10 inches in length.

343 Arrow crabs are a species of marine crab. They inhabit different parts of the world, including the Caribbean, Indo-Pacific region, California, and eastern Africa. It resembles a spider with its long legs. The only way to tell if it is a crab or spider is by counting its legs—crabs have ten legs, whereas a spider only has 8.

INSECTS AND CRUSTACEANS

344

A group of small crustaceans that are found in the sea are called copepods. They can be found in almost every freshwater habitat. They range between 0.5 millimetres to 5 millimetres in length. One of the copepods is known as cyclops because of it has one eye, just like the Greek and Roman mythological creature.

345
Insects do not breathe like human beings with their lungs. They breathe through holes in their exoskeletons called spiracles. Insects have these spiracles in a line along their thoraxes and abdomens, which makes it seem as if they are breathing through their sides.

346
The circulatory system of insects is also different from mammals. They do not have arteries and veins carrying blood inside their bodies. Instead, their circulatory system is open and the blood bathes the organs. Their blood is called 'hemolymph' which is typically clear but can also be greenish or yellowish in colour.

SPECIES, CHARACTERISTICS AND HABITAT

347 The oldest fossil of an insect was found to be some 400 million years old. It was a set of jaws of an insect. The fossil thus showed that insects were among the first animals that have made the transition from sea to land. It also suggests that insects were crawling on the planet some 170 million years before dinosaurs came into being.

348 Meganeuropsis, which is also known as the Griffinfly, lived around 290 million years ago. It was the largest insect ever known, with a wingspan of 2.5 feet. These ancient dragonflies terrorised the skies for several years. They preyed on other small insects and on small amphibians as well.

349 Insects have compound eyes that are made up of many individual visual units called ommatidia. A common misconception regarding the ommatidia is that each unit acts as its own eye. Actually, it acts more like pixels that build up into a mosaic imagery.

INSECTS AND CRUSTACEANS

350 Onthophagus taurus, which is commonly known as a horned dung beetle, is the strongest insect on the planet. It is also called the bull-headed dung beetle and taurus scarab. According to scientists, this dung beetle can pull 1,141 times its own body weight.

351 An unusual fact about mosquitoes is that they tend to bite more when there is a full moon. Although scientists have not been able to give an actual reason for this, but it has been observed that they can bite up to 500 per cent more during a full moon.

352 Insects do not have tongues like humans. Most of them taste their food with their antennae or their mouthparts. But did you know that butterflies taste with their feet? They land on their food and the special chemical receptors in their feet find out the taste of the food before consuming it.

SPECIES, CHARACTERISTICS AND HABITAT

353 There are many insects that can glow, but fireflies are the only insects that can flash their lights on and off. They do it because they have a compound called luciferin in their bodies. When it comes in contact with air, it glows.

354 Fireflies warn their predators to stay away by flashing their lights. Some of the fireflies have their own pattern of flashing lights, just like having their own language. One species, which is called synchronous fireflies, flash their lights in unison during a two-week long mating season.

355 When food is scarce, lobsters can turn into cannibals and eat smaller lobsters. Lobsters are also sometimes called 'bugs' because the nervous system of the crustacean is similar to that of bugs like grasshoppers and ants.

INSECTS AND CRUSTACEANS

356 The beautiful orange and black monarch butterfly is the most easily recognisable butterfly in the world. The North American monarchs take part in the most amazing migration, covering 2,000 miles a year and always picking their ancestor's trees! No one knows how these butterflies recognise their migratory path, since they only live a few months and cannot teach their young.

357 Dung beetles are not known for their 'fancy' abode! They eat and often live in dung. Adult dung beetles eat the liquid part of the dung, while the young or larvae eat the solid. In fact, the dung's undigested content offers sufficient nutrition for these beetles. Some carry it out, some tunnel beneath, while some live inside the dung!

358 The cicadas' shrill buzzing sound comes from the plates on their abdomen, which they vibrate during mating season or when under threat. In a swarm, this noise can reach 120 decibels, louder than a chainsaw! There are roughly 3,000 species of cicadas. These are divided into two kinds: annual cicadas and periodical cicadas.

SPECIES, CHARACTERISTICS AND HABITAT

359 The annual cicadas appear every year, while the periodical cicadas appear every 13 or 17 years. The periodical cicadas are found in the United States. Their life begins when the female lays eggs on trees. On hatching the young, known as nymphs, drop to the ground. They immediately burrow underground, emerging as they hit adulthood—every 13 or 17 years.

360 Cockroaches are one of the most primitive creatures on Earth today. They go back hundreds of millions of years, and were probably present when the dinosaurs ruled Earth. Although we think of cockroaches as pests, only 30 out of 4,000 of its species fall under the category. They can eat almost anything and can live for a long time without any food! In fact, they can stay alive even if their head is cut off.

361 Known for its hissing sound, the Madagascar hissing cockroach is unlike any other cockroach. For instance, it has no wings and only a single antenna. The males also have distinct horns which they use when fighting with other males. The hissing is also a powerful tool. In a fight between two cockroaches, the one with the louder hiss wins!

INSECTS AND CRUSTACEANS

362 **The stick insect can hold a master class in mimicry.** Also called walking sticks, the colouring of the stick Insects almost exactly matches its surrounding. Thus, they are usually green, brown or black, while some are even multi-coloured. When a predator grabs them by a limb, they simply shed that leg and scuttle away. Later they re-grow the limb. Stick insects can vary in size from half an inch, to the 21 inches long phobaeticus kirbyi, the world's longest insect!

363 **The praying mantis gets its name from its long front legs which it holds together at the front, giving it an appearance of praying.** The praying Mantis also excels at camouflage, and is coloured according to its habitat. Some mantises are also found in unusual shapes, resembling branches or leaves. As a carnivorous insect feeding on other smaller bugs, the praying mantis is a farmer's friend. This carnivorous insect can turn its head 180°!

364 **Domesticated for the silk threads they produce, the silkworm is no longer found in the wild.** It is actually the caterpillar form of a moth. The larva eats mulberry leaves constantly. It then attaches itself to a stick, spinning a cocoon of raw silk that it makes in its mouth. It takes roughly 5,000 such cocoons to make a pound of silk. After centuries of domestication, the silkworm has lost some of its traits. The larva's legs have degenerated and the adult moth has lost its ability to fly.

SPECIES, CHARACTERISTICS AND HABITAT

365

The banded wooly bear caterpillar is found in the extremely cold regions of the Arctic circle. This has forced some unique adaptive features in the caterpillar. As the winter starts to set in, the caterpillar freezes itself. It produces an antifreeze substance that protects its brain, organs and heart even as it almost stops beating. Then, in spring it thaws and continues to eat. The banded wooly bear caterpillar has an unusually long life among insects—14 years.

366

The beautiful swallowtail is found in a range of habitats across the world, although their population is dwindling. This butterfly has a stunning pattern of black on a pale yellow base with a red spot and blue shade on the hind wings. Although the butterfly looks so stunning, the caterpillar looks like a bird dropping which is an excellent camouflage.

367

In the rain forests of Costa Rica, there exists a unique relationship between acacia ants and the acacia tree. Where ivy plants easily creep up to block the sunlight for most plants, in the case of the acacia tree, these ants intervene by cutting and throwing away the ivy! The acacia ant even protects the tree from big invaders like goats by stinging them. In return the plant rewards them with nutrients and shelter.

INSECTS AND CRUSTACEANS

368 **Did you know that you carry many insects on your own body?** In fact, almost all warm-blooded birds and animals carry these insects. A commonly found insect is the Wingless Lice. There are almost 5,000 different species of lice. Chewing lice feed on skin and debris, while sucking lice feed on blood and other secretions. Humans host three types of lice—head lice, body lice and pubic lice.

369 **With black dots on a bright red background, the ladybug is certainly eye-catching.** But the colouring is also an excellent deterrent, warning predators to stay away. Ladybugs are also known as farmer's friends because they feed vicariously on aphids. It lays its eggs in an aphid's nest and on hatching, the ladybug larvae immediately start feeding on them.

370 **The luna moth has a remarkable wingspan—almost four inches in width and five inches in length.** Found mostly in the US and Canada, the luna moth is also remarkable for its appetite. Although the caterpillar will munch almost constantly, the adult moth has no appetite. In fact, it has no mouth or digestive system and lives only a week!

SPECIES, CHARACTERISTICS AND HABITAT

371 Closely related to the honeybee, the bumblebee also collect nectar from flowers and live in a highly hierarchal society. Bumblebees build their nest from piles of leaves on the ground. The nests will have close to 400 bees that are divided into worker bees, drones and the queen. It is the worker bees that collect nectar and feed the rest. Unlike the honeybee, the bumblebee does not die after stinging.

372 Carpenter bees closely resemble and are often mistaken for the bumblebee. Carpenter bees get their name from their habit of building their nest by burrowing into hard wooden material like window frames. Unlike bumblebees, most carpenter bee species are solitary. However, the solitary bees are quite friendly, often building their nests close to each other! Did you know that only the female carpenter bee can sting? However, they only do this under extreme provocation.

373 Unlike bees, wasps can sting repeatedly. But most wasps are actually quite harmless, an only sting in defence. This is a diverse species and contains bees of all sizes and colours, including red, metallic blue and the more familiar yellow. They can either be solitary or social. Social species build massive colonies with close to 5,000 wasps!

INSECTS AND CRUSTACEANS

374

The dragonfly is one of the most ancient insects on Earth, existing even before the dinosaurs. The larval dragonfly is aquatic and eats almost everything around it, including fish, tadpoles and other insects. The adult dragonfly, on the other hand, is an incredible flying creature. It can hover, go up and down and even mate in mid-air. The globe skinner dragonfly travels 11,000 miles across the Indian Ocean, the longest migration route among insects.

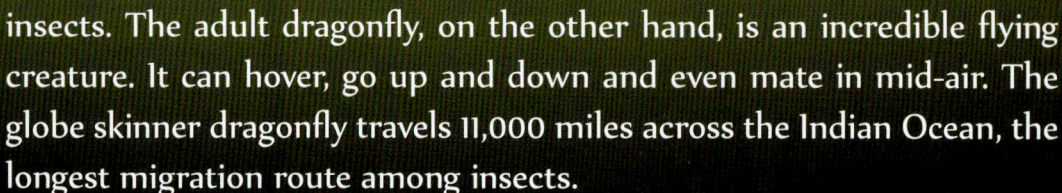

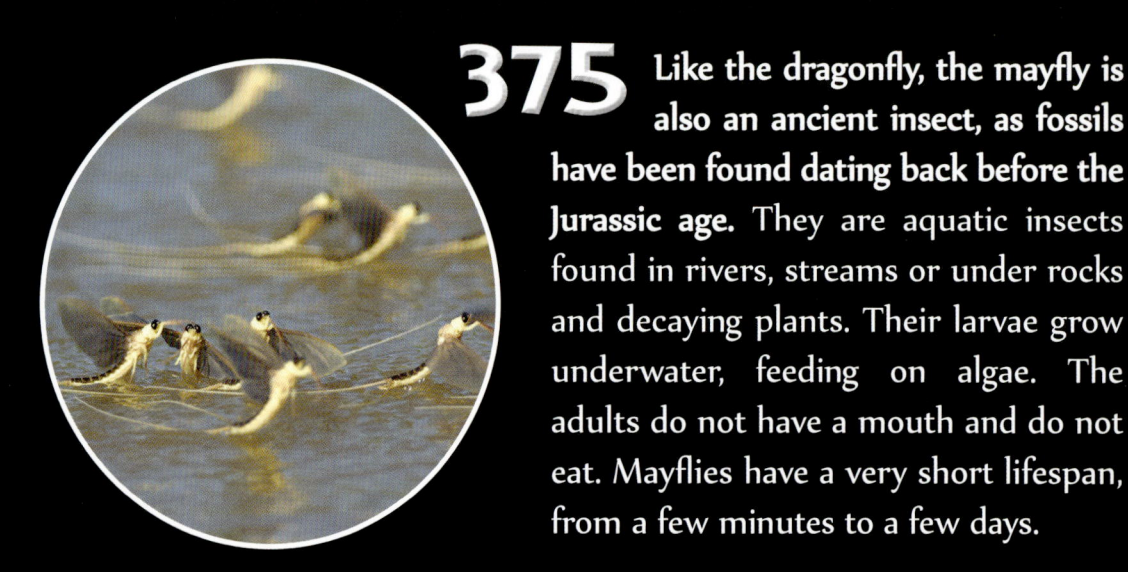

375
Like the dragonfly, the mayfly is also an ancient insect, as fossils have been found dating back before the Jurassic age. They are aquatic insects found in rivers, streams or under rocks and decaying plants. Their larvae grow underwater, feeding on algae. The adults do not have a mouth and do not eat. Mayflies have a very short lifespan, from a few minutes to a few days.

376
The kissing bug, or the assassin bug, is a carrier of chagas disease. It is called so because it bites just next to a person's lips. The bug leaves a wound with the bite, causing a parasitic infection. The Bugs themselves have an immune system that is modified to withstand the parasite.

SPECIES, CHARACTERISTICS AND HABITAT

377 There are many species of fruit fly. Fruit flies are named so because they are attracted to ripe or rotting fruit. They will attack fruits, eat leaves or burrow in stems, causing considerable damage. Some examples are the Mexican fly that targets citrus crops, and the olive fruit fly that attacks olives in the Mediterranean region.

378 Despite its name, the velvet ant is not actually an ant. It's a wasp! The male velvet ant has wings to fly, but the female does not. These wasps have colourful velvet-like hair, earning them their name. The females have a formidable array of defensive tools, such as a hard body and a potent and toxic sting.

379 The weaver ants are known for their amazing nest building skills. Worker ants work together to bring together leaves and then use the larva to produce silk. This silk is then used to weave together the leaves, producing a nest. Weaver ants build colonies, some of which are large enough to include a hundred nests and millions of ants!

380 **The fire ant is actually a common name for more than 200 different species.** They get their name from their powerful sting, which is compared to a fire burn. Fire ants live in large mounds on the ground, forming colonies. They are omnivorous and will even eat small animals. These invasive insects are aggressive and extremely territorial.

381 **Stink bugs get their name from the foul odour they release when threatened.** They are native to China, Japan and Taiwan. They are considered pests because they feed on agricultural crops and fruits. Stink bugs like warmer temperatures and will go into hibernation in winters.

382 **There are 23 species of tsetse fly, all of which are native to Africa.** These flies have lived almost unchanged on Earth for more than 34 million years. They feed on the blood of humans and animals. The tsetse fly is considered extremely dangerous because it transmits fatal parasitic infections among humans and animals. Two species of the tsetse fly are even known to be responsible for sleeping sleep sickness among humans.

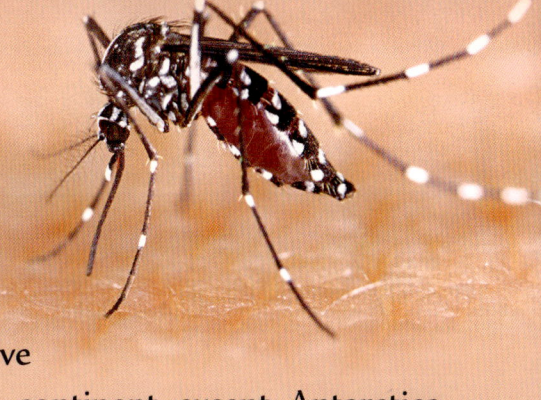

SPECIES, CHARACTERISTICS AND HABITAT

383 **The aedes mosquito is notorious for its ability to transmit serious diseases among humans, such as chikungunya, dengue, zika virus and yellow fever.** Native to tropic and subtropical regions, these invasive mosquitoes are now found on every continent except Antarctica. Unlike other mosquitoes, they bite during the day, especially at dawn and dusk.

384 **There are 3,106 species of termites, with hundreds of species not yet described!** They are also called 'silent killers' because they seem to feed on almost anything, destroying human homes and property. Termites feed on debris like dead wood, paper, plastic and even walls! Termites are found in all continents of earth, except Antarctica.

385 **Termites live in large colonies that can range from a few hundreds, to several millions of individuals.** Like wasps and bees, they have a clearly defined hierachial society with workers, soldiers, king and queen. Termite queens have the longest lifespan among insects, some living as long as 30 to 50 years.

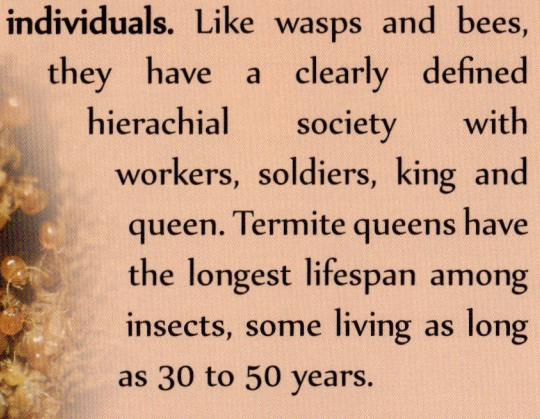

INSECTS AND CRUSTACEANS

386 There are many species of bed bugs of which the common bed bug prefer feeding on human blood. Other species prefer other animals. The insect gets its name from its preference for a warm environment like warm beds and beddings. They feed at an interval of five to ten days and can survive for months without food.

387 **Most bugs have a preference when it comes to the source of their food.** For example, the western conifer seed bug only feeds on the developing cones and seeds of conifers. The Mexican bean beetle likes to snack on beans, from lima beans to mung beans. Bat bugs, on the other hand, prefer to suck bat's blood.

388 **The earwig gets its name from a myth that they crawl into people's ears and tunnel into their brain to lay eggs while they are sleeping!** There are 2,000 species of earwigs and they are found in every continent except Antarctica. They have short forewings and a pair of skin-like hindwings. In fact, its scientific name means 'skin wings'.

SPECIES, CHARACTERISTICS AND HABITAT

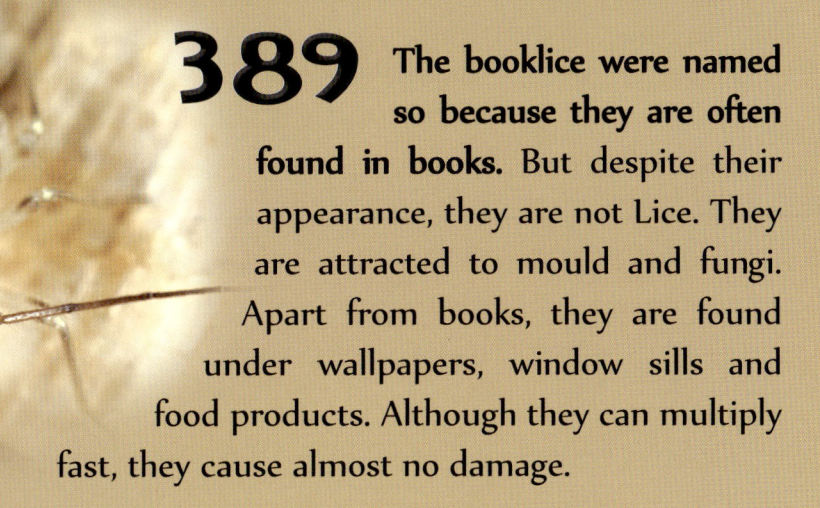

389 The booklice were named so because they are often found in books. But despite their appearance, they are not Lice. They are attracted to mould and fungi. Apart from books, they are found under wallpapers, window sills and food products. Although they can multiply fast, they cause almost no damage.

390 The giant mesquite bug is, in fact, quite large and noticeable. Its name also comes from its preference for the mesquite tree. The insect is very vividly coloured, bright red with white lines and dots. The colouration makes it vulnerable to predators. But the bug emits a foul smell that keeps them at bay.

391 The scale insect secrets a waxy substance to coat its body as a defence mechanism. This waxy material has the appearance of a fish's scales, giving the insect its unique name. There are about 8,000 different species of scale insects. These insects are plant parasites and feed on a plant's sap.

INSECTS AND CRUSTACEANS

392 The snakefly is considered a living fossil! A living fossil is a species that seems very similar to an organism only found as fossil. It got its name because its appearance and behaviour often resembles a snake. It has a flattened head with a long neck, which is actually a thorax, giving it the appearance of a snake. It can also raise its neck above its body like a snake. It is considered beneficial for humans because it feeds on other pest insects like aphids.

393 The longhorn beetle gets name from its unusually long antennae, sometimes longer than its body. There are 26,000 species of longhorn beetles. Most of these have vivid colouring. Many of the species are extremely invasive and are considered pests. The larvae tunnel into wood, whether living or dead, causing massive damage.

394 Among the most destructive of pests when it comes to humans are the weevil beetles. There are over 60,000 species of the weevil beetle. Different species of this beetle, such as the rice beetle, maize beetle and granary beetle, attack seeds and grains, including stored grains. This ability of destruction is used to our advantage by using them to kill invasive plants.

SPECIES, CHARACTERISTICS AND HABITAT

395 **The skin beetle (also known as carpet or leather beetle) is a beneficial scavenger.** It feeds on dead animals or plants. Usually skin beetles start their work when the dead body is drying out. It may sound gruesome, but they are very essential for the environment because they clean up skin, hair and muscles from a dying body.

396 **The Dobsonfly is one of the largest insects known.** It is found in Asia, South Africa and the Americas. The dobsonfly larvae live at the rocky bottom of a stream, while the adults are also usually also found near streams. The larva is an aggressive predator, but the adults live only for a week and do not eat anything. The dobsonfly larva does not like polluted water. So, any stream with the larvae is usually clear and safe.

397 **The caddisfly is a close relative of moths and butterflies. It has four hairy wings.** The caddisfly larva is aquatic. It is found near freshwater habitats around the world. Some caddisfly species are herbivorous, some carnivorous, while others are omnivorous. Some species produce silk. Most larvae create a case for their protection and drag it around with their body.

INSECTS AND CRUSTACEANS

398 The most common insect and the one most familiar to us is the housefly. Houseflies depend on humans and their domesticated animals for their very survival. Hence, they are found wherever humans have formed habitats. Houseflies like to feed and reproduce in garbage. This also makes them a dangerous carrier of diseases as they carry germs from the garbage to our food.

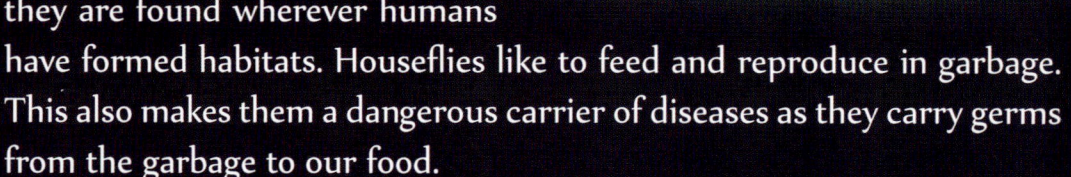

399 The housefly's wings beat up to 1,000 times a minute! Despite this, it is quite slow and rarely moves unless compelled to. The housefly has compound eyes with 4,000 lenses in each eye. This gives them the ability to view several pictures at the same time. Did you know that a housefly tastes with its feet? This is because its taste receptors are located in its feet.

400 Also known as greenflies and plant lice, aphids are considered serious pests for crops. They can multiply rapidly and cause significant damage to crops. There are roughly 4,400 known aphid species. Aphids attach themselves to plants and suck out their sap. The excess liquid is removed in the form of a sticky liquid which is called honeydew. Aphids often share a symbiotic relationship with ants, who give them shelter and protect them from predators. In return the ant feeds on the aphid's honeydew.

EXTINCT ANIMALS

Details of Extinct Animals

401 The golden toad was a small fluorescent amphibian that was last sighted in 1989. The International Union for Conservation of Nature (IUCN) has now classified it as an extinct animal. It is said to have become extinct due to global warming, rising pollution, and fungal skin infections.

402 A black-faced honeycreeper, po'ouli, is a species of bird that is native to the island of Maui in Hawaii. The bird has a black head, brown upper parts, and pale grey underparts. It was discovered in the 1970s, but their population started declining rapidly. By 1997, only three birds of the species were left, and seven years later it was declared extinct.

403 The tecopa pupfish was a small, heat-tolerant fish that was native to the hot springs in the Mojave Desert of California. These fish were about 1 to 1.5 inches long. In the 1970s, habitat modifications and introduction of non-native species led to its extinction.

EXTINCT ANIMALS

404 **One of the sub-species of the Spanish Ibex was the Pyrenean ibex.** Commonly found in the Cantabrian Mountains, Southern France, and the northern Pyrenees, this species became extinct in 2000. The last Pyrenean ibex was a female called Celia.

405 **The Iberian ibex had four sub-species.** The first sub-species to become extinct was the Portuguese ibex, which was declared extinct as early as 1892. After the last Pyrenean Ibex, Celia, was found dead on 6 January 2000, scientists tried to clone the ibex from the skin samples of Celia. However, this cloned ibex died shortly after being born.

406 **The West African black rhinoceros was one of the sub-species of the black rhinoceros.** The International Union for Conservation of Nature (IUCN) declared the species extinct in 2011. The main cause of their extinction was killing of these rhinos by poachers for their horns.

DETAILS OF EXTINCT ANIMALS

407 In the valleys of the Laurisilva forests on Portugal's Madeira Islands, there lived a species of butterfly known as the Madeiran large white butterfly. It had pure white wings with the tip of the forewings tinted black. This large white butterfly was commonly found across Europe, Asia, and Africa.

408 **The Madeiran Large White Butterfly was last collected in 1977, but surveys in the 1980s and 1990s could not collect any more of this species.** The International Union for Conservation of Nature (IUCN) has listed them as critically endangered and possibly extinct. The main causes for their extinction are believed to be the rise of pollution and loss of habitat due to construction. There are also suggestions that a virus outbreak might have wiped out the population of this butterfly.

409 **The Javan Tiger inhabited the Indonesian island of Java until the mid-1970s.** It was one of the sub-species of the tiger and one of the three sub-species limited to islands. A severe population decline took place due to the loss of habitat and agricultural development. Although there were some conservation efforts made in the 1940s and 50s, the tiger became extinct due to the lack of adequate land and planning.

159

EXTINCT ANIMALS

410 There is an extinct species of snake known as the round island burrowing boa. This snake species was native to Mauritius and was last seen on round island in 1975. After its extinction, no other sub-species of this reptile has been recognised. The main cause of its extinction is said to be the introduction of non-native species of rabbit and goats that destroyed vegetation and also the boa's habitat.

411 Sabre-toothed cats were felines that became extinct about 12,000 years ago. They were often called sabre-toothed tigers or sabre-toothed lions. They were carnivorous and had elongated canine teeth that were, in some cases, about 50 centimetres long. One of the main causes of their extinctions was the climatic change of the Earth.

412 An extinct mammal that is said to be closely related to the present-day elephant was the woolly mammoth. These creatures weighed over six tonnes and were over four metres tall. They had fur all over their body and had large curved tusks that were up to five metres long.

DETAILS OF EXTINCT ANIMALS

413 **The woolly mammoths disappeared around 10,000 years ago. They roamed the Earth during the Ice Age.** The shift in weather conditions and warming up of the Earth changed their natural habitat and food supply, and led to their extinction. We know about them from prehistoric cave paintings and fossilised remains.

414 **Found mainly in the grasslands of the Netherlands, the Dutch alcon blue butterfly is said to have been a sub-species of the alcon blue butterfly.** It was native to parts of Europe and Asia but was last seen in 1979. The causes of its extinction were the increase in farming and building, which had adverse effects on its habitat and resulted in the loss of its main food source.

415 **Spix's macaw was known for its beautiful blue feathers and was endemic to Brazil.** It was also called the Little blue macaw. It belonged to the parrot family and is today considered critically endangered by the IUCN. They are extinct in the wild, and only a few of these parrots are alive in captivity. Their extinction was caused due to habitat destruction and illegal trade and trapping.

EXTINCT ANIMALS

416 A flightless bird, dodo, was native to the island of Mauritius, east of Madagascar in the Indian Ocean. The bird belonged to the family of pigeons and doves. The last appearance of dodo was in the drawings and writings from the 17th century.

417 The dodo is believed to have been one metre tall and around 10–18 kilograms in weight. While we have some drawings, its exact appearance remains a mystery due to its varied illustrations from the 17th century. The main cause of its extinction is believed to be hunting by sailors. The last sighting of the bird is said have been in 1662.

418 The Steller's sea cow was endemic to the North Pacific Ocean. It was a herbivorous marine animal. It was also among the largest mammals, other than Whales, during the ancient period, as it was about nine metres in length. The Steller's sea cows were hunted to extinction and last reported alive in 1768.

DETAILS OF EXTINCT ANIMALS

419

Tasmanian tigers were native to Australia, Tasmania, and New Guinea. They were not related to tigers, but were large carnivorous marsupials. They seemed to resemble large sized dogs and weighed around 30 kilograms. They had dark stripes on their body that gave them the appearance of a tiger. They became extinct around 1982 due to excessive hunting as well as human encroachment into their habitats, and spread of diseases.

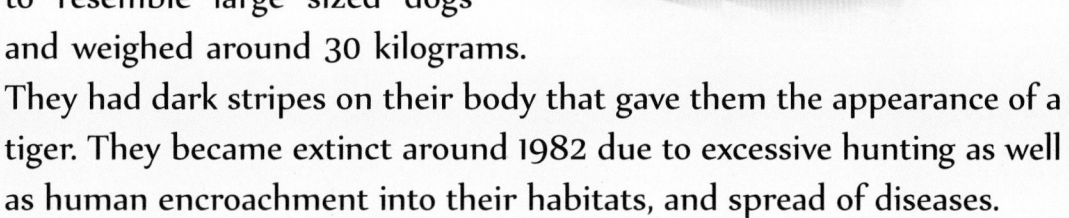

420 Great auks were large flightless birds that were found in North Atlantic and Northern Spain. They weighed around five kilograms and were good swimmers. They used to hunt for food under water. During 1835, the last colony of auks was said to have been living on the island of Eldey until they were all killed.

421 The great auks were not related to penguins, but they were the first birds that were called penguins. They had white bellies and black coloured backs. It is said that in 1844, the last three birds were killed by three men in Scotland. During a large storm the men thought these birds to be witches causing the storm, and hence they killed them.

163

EXTINCT ANIMALS

422 There was a species of pigeon known as the passenger pigeon or wild pigeon that is now extinct. Its name was derived from the French word 'passager' which means 'passing by'. This pigeon was native to North America and was given this name due to its migratory nature. The passenger pigeons have been extinct since the early 20th century.

423 It is said that when Europeans arrived in North America, three to five billion passenger pigeons inhabited the US. However, after the settlement, the North American continent faced mass deforestation which led to habitat loss and decreased the bird population. Also, it was in the 19th century that pigeon meat became common food for the poor and its hunting became one of the main causes for its extinction. The last of these pigeons died in 1914 in captivity.

424 A species of freshwater dolphin, the baiji white dolphin, was native to the Yangtze River in China for about 20 million years. They were the first dolphin species to become extinct. These dolphins could grow to be up to eight feet long. They weighed up to a quarter of ton and due to their tiny eyes, they had very poor eyesight.

DETAILS OF EXTINCT ANIMALS

425 **The numbers of the baiji white dolphins declined drastically after the 1950s.** The main cause for this decline was the growing industrialisation in China which had an adverse effect on the rivers. Although the IUCN had declared the dolphins as critically endangered, after 2002 no dolphins have been sighted and they are believed to be extinct.

426 **The Irish elk is an extinct species of deer, also known as the Irish giant deer.** It was one of the largest Deer that ever existed. It was found around Eurasia, Ireland, Siberia, and China. It is not related to the present-day family of elk, which is called Moose in North America.

427 **The Irish elk could grow up to seven feet tall and weighed around 700 kilograms.** They had huge antlers, the largest of any of the deer species, around 12 feet in width. They became extinct in about 5,200 BC. It is believed that hunting by humans was the main cause of their extinction. Apart from hunting, the changing weather of the planet also contributed in an adverse manner, as the change in climate and plant life affected the available food sources.

EXTINCT ANIMALS

428 The quagga lived in South Africa until the 19th century when it became extinct. It was a sub-species of plains zebra. In appearance, the quagga looked like half-zebra and half-horse. It got its name from the sound that it made. Only 23 skins of the quagga are preserved, whereas only one live quagga has ever been photographed.

429 The quagga were around four feet tall and eight feet long. Not much is known about their behaviour as they lived in the wild. Quaggas were hunted to extinction for their meat and also to preserve the land for agriculture. The last quagga died in captivity in Amsterdam on 12 August 1883.

430 The Japanese Honshu wolf was a sub-species of the grey wolf. It was endemic to the Japanese region, especially in the islands of Honshu, Shikoku, and Kyushu. It was one of the two species of wolf that were found in the Japanese region. Due to deforestation, their habitat was disturbed and they were hunted until their extinction in 1905.

DETAILS OF EXTINCT ANIMALS

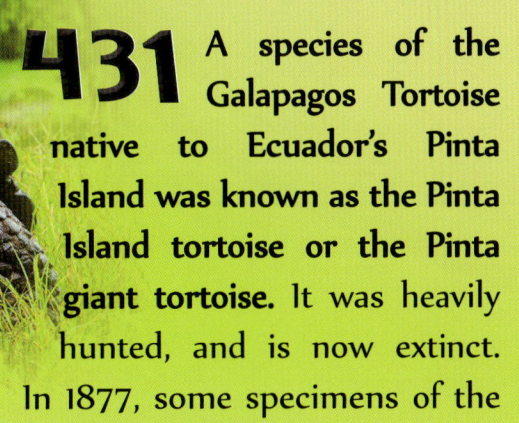

431 A species of the Galapagos Tortoise native to Ecuador's Pinta Island was known as the Pinta Island tortoise or the Pinta giant tortoise. It was heavily hunted, and is now extinct. In 1877, some specimens of the tortoise were brought to London but by the end of the 19th century, most of these tortoises had died out.

432 The Pinta Island tortoises were hunted mainly for food during the 19th century. In the 1950s, their habitat was destroyed when goats were introduced to the island. By 1971, only one tortoise was left, although attempts were made to conserve many of them. This famous tortoise, named Lonesome George, was the only one of his kind until he died in 2012.

433 The moa was a huge flightless bird endemic to New Zealand. It could grow up to 12 feet in height and weighed around 230 kilograms. This species was hunted by Haast's Eagle and later on by humans as well. It became extinct in around 1400 AD.

EXTINCT ANIMALS

434 The moa was a huge bird with its neck pointed forward. It is believed that their long necks produced low pitched sounds. The Māori people arrived in New Zealand around 1300 CE and started hunting the bird. Unfortunately, in less than a century the species became extinct due to this relentless hunting.

435 The Maori people called the Haast's eagle 'Pouakai', which means a monstrous bird. It was a huge bird with a wingspan of two to three metres. It weighed up to 13 kilograms and is the largest eagle ever to have existed. They became extinct around 1500 AD, after the Maori people arrived in New Zealand.

436 In the Maori legend, the Haast's eagle is believed to prey on animals and humans. Looking at its size, it is possible that the eagle preyed on humans as it easily hunted the moa that were huge and much heavier than humans. Soon after the moa became extinct, the population of these eagles also diminished due to the lack of their main food. Humans also hunted them, which finally resulted in their extinction.

DETAILS OF EXTINCT ANIMALS

437 An extinct species of lemurs, the megaladapis, which was informally known as koala lemur, was native to the island of madagascar. The largest of this species measured four to five feet in length. The Megaladapis had a build that was similar to the modern koala and it was quite different from any living lemur we see nowadays. Forest fires and habitat destruction caused their extinction around 1420 AD.

438 Sivatherium, which means Lord Shiva's beast, is an extinct animal that was closely related to the present-day giraffe. It lived throughout Africa and the Indian subcontinent. It had a wide antler-like pair of ossicones on its head and another pair of small ossicones above its eyes. It became extinct around 6000 BC.

439 Another tiger sub-species that is extinct now is the Caspian tiger. It is also called the hyrcanian tiger and turan Tiger. It was living in the wild until the end of the 20th century when it was declared extinct. It is believed to be one of the biggest cats to have ever lived on Earth. Hunting and poaching are the main reasons for its extinction.

EXTINCT ANIMALS

440 A sub-species of the lizard that is now extinct was called the Roque Chico de Salmor giant lizard. It was native to the Canary Islands and disappeared into extinction during the 1930s. The main cause for its extinction was its predation by the cats and carnivorous birds.

441 An extinct species of rhinoceros that was native to Eurasia was the Elasmotherium. It was the size of a mammoth and had a large thick horn on its forehead. It was also known as the giant rhinoceros or giant Siberian unicorn. The legs of the animal were adapted for galloping, which gave it a horse-like gait. It became extinct at around 10,000 BC.

442 The megatapirus, also known as the giant tapir, was endemic to southern China and Vietnam. It was larger than the present-day tapirs, at about three feet tall and seven feet long. It weighed around 500 kilograms. The megatapirus became extinct around 2000 BC.

DETAILS OF EXTINCT ANIMALS

443

A sub-species of the clouded leopard that was endemic to the island of Taiwan was the Formosan clouded leopard that became extinct during the 1990s. It was the second-largest carnivore in Taiwan during its lifetime, after the Formosan black bear. Poaching and habitat destruction were the two main reasons that drove it to extinction.

444

The Eurasian wild horse, also known as tarpan, was found in Europe and was a sub-species of the wild horse. In 1909, the last of these horses died in captivity in Russia. Several attempts were made to develop horses that could resemble tarpans by selective breeding. These attempts were started during the 1930s but none managed to look exactly like the real tarpan.

445

The pied raven is a sub-species of the common raven and was a native to the Faroe Islands in Denmark. It had large white areas on its head, wings, and belly. The beak of the pied raven is brown coloured. Other than its white areas, it looked like any common raven in size and shape. Unfortunately, they were hunted to extinction. The last pied raven was seen in 1948.

EXTINCT ANIMALS

446

An extinct freshwater fish was the Gravenche, which was also known as the Lake Geneva Whitefish or 'Little Fera'. It lived in Lake Geneva in Switzerland and France. It could reach a length between 25 to 32 centimetres. Due to overfishing, the Gravenche became extinct during the 1950s.

447

Caddisflies are small moth-like creatures. One of its species was the Tobias' caddisfly which is now extinct. It lived on the River Rhine between Mainz and Cologne in Germany. The River Rhine has been polluted by the industrial waste for decades now, and many of the caddisfly species have become extinct due to the polluted river. Tobias' caddisfly was last seen in 1983.

448

The deer family had a sub-species by the name of the Schomburgk's deer that was endemic to central Thailand. It was named after Sir Robert H. Schomburgk who was the British consul in Bangkok from 1857–1864. Loss of habitat and hunting of the species drove them to extinction and the last of the species was killed in captivity in 1938.

DETAILS OF EXTINCT ANIMALS

449 In the 1970s, an aquatic mammal became extinct. This was the Japanese sea lion, which was initially considered to be a sub-species of the California sea lion, but subsequently was reclassified as a separate species. During World War-II, submarine warfare contributed to their habitat destruction. Added to this, over-hunting also became a major cause of their extinction. The last confirmed Japanese sea lion was captured in 1974.

450 During the mid-20th century, the Arabian ostrich or the Syrian ostrich became extinct from the Middle East. It was a sub-species of the ostrich. The introduction of motor vehicles and firearms initiated the decline of the species. The Arabian ostriches were declared extinct in 1966.

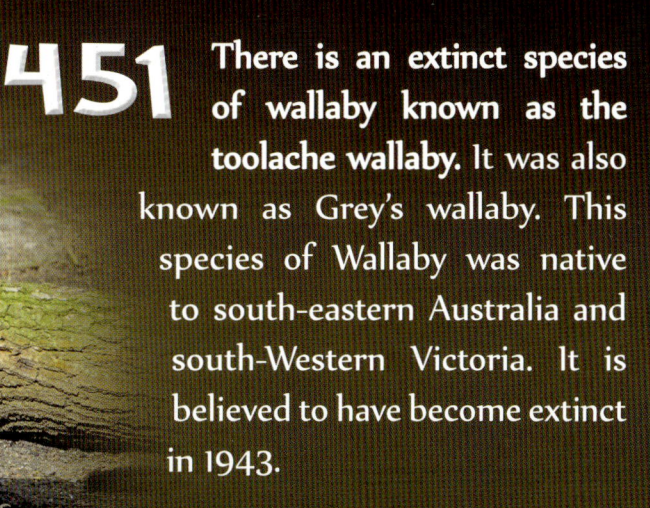

451 There is an extinct species of wallaby known as the toolache wallaby. It was also known as Grey's wallaby. This species of Wallaby was native to south-eastern Australia and south-Western Victoria. It is believed to have become extinct in 1943.

EXTINCT ANIMALS

452 During the 1920s, an effort was made to conserve the remaining toolache wallabies from the brink of extinction. It was decided to keep the last known species in captivity to protect them, but the effort ended in a disaster when 10 out of the 14 wallabies died during this process.

453 The Antillean giant rice rat, which is also known as megalomys desmarestii, was native to Martinique in the Caribbean. It was as big as a cat and also knew how to swim. The rat became extinct due to the eruption of the volcano Mount Pelée in 1902 and also because it was hunted by its natural predator, mongoose, during that time.

454 An extinct species of the common raccoon was the Barbados raccoon that was native to Barbados in North America. The last sighting of the Barbados raccoon took place in 1964 when one specimen was killed by a car on a road. The species was declared extinct by the IUCN in 1996. Tourism and habitat destruction are the main causes for the extinction of the Barbados raccoon.

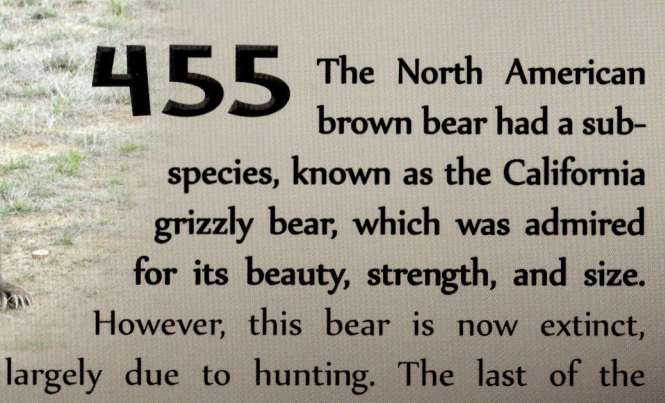

DETAILS OF EXTINCT ANIMALS

455 The North American brown bear had a sub-species, known as the California grizzly bear, which was admired for its beauty, strength, and size. However, this bear is now extinct, largely due to hunting. The last of the California grizzly bears were seen in 1924 and thereafter, were labelled extinct.

456 The Caribbean Monk Seal became extinct in 1952. It was also known as the West Indian seal or sea wolf. The two main predators of the Caribbean monk seal were sharks and humans. Hunting and killing of the seals by humans, mainly to obtain the oil held within their blubber, led the species towards extinction.

457 A sub-species of grey wolf, the Newfoundland wolf, was endemic to Newfoundland, Canada. It was a medium-sized wolf with a slender skull and a white pelt. In 1911, the last Newfoundland wolf was reportedly killed. Since then it has been labelled as one of the extinct animals on the planet.

EXTINCT ANIMALS

458 Dr. H.E. Anthony excavated a skull fragment of the Puerto Rico long-nosed bat in the large Cathedral Cave near Morovis, Puerto Rico. This sub-species of bat had never been observed or even documented live. It is believed that the main cause of its extinction was the frequent hurricanes in the area.

459

The sea mink belonged to the family of Mustelidae and became extinct during 1860–1870. It was commonly found in Atlantic Canada and New England in North Eastern America. The main cause for the extinction of the sea mink was hunting due to demand for their fur in the European market.

460 Euceratherium or the shrub-ox was a species of Bovidae that was endemic to North America. In fact, it was among the first bovids that entered North America. The shrub-ox had a massive build and was believed to follow a diet of trees and shrubs. It became extinct around 9500 BC.

DETAILS OF EXTINCT ANIMALS

461 The tule shrew was native to Baja California, Mexico, and was a sub-species of the ornate shrew of North America. The upper parts and sides of the tule shrew were grey or slightly darker than the ornate shrew. It is said to have become extinct by 1905.

462 A goose-sized sea duck, chendytes lawi, was a flightless bird that was common in the Western US coastal area. Humans exploited this flightless bird for around 8,000 years, which is probably the most humans have ever exploited any animal so far. It is believed to have become extinct between 450–250 BC due to human hunting, habitat destruction and animal predation.

463 A species of ciconia was the ciconia maltha, which is also called asphalt stork or La Brea stork. It was a large species of ciconia having a height of over four feet and wingspan of about nine feet across. It was native to the Western and Southern USA and Cuba. It became extinct in 10,000 BC.

EXTINCT ANIMALS

464 An extinct flightless barn owl was the tyto pollens, which was also known as the Bahamian barn owl or chickcharney. It was a burrow-nesting owl that lived in the pineyards of Andros Island in the Bahamas. In the 16th century, the island was colonised by the Europeans and the forests were felled. Due to the habitat destruction, the species became extinct.

465 The Jamaica giant galliwasp was endemic to Jamaica and belonged to the species of lizard. It was last seen in 1840 and is said to have become extinct since then. One of the main causes for its extinction was the introduction of predators like mongooses.

466 The Ecnomiohyla rabborum is commonly known as Rabbs' fringe-limbed treefrog. It was endemic to Panama and was a relatively large frog. The species was first discovered in 2005, but was declared extinct on 26 September 2016.

DETAILS OF EXTINCT ANIMALS

467 **The Rabbs' fringe-limbed treefrog glided by spreading its huge webbed hands and feet during descent.** The males of this species were very responsible and guarded the young. They even provided food for the young. This was the only known species of frogs where the tadpoles got their nutrition by feeding on the skin cells of their fathers.

468 **Oncorhynchus rastrosus is also known as the sabretooth salmon.** It is an extinct species of fish. It is believed to have become extinct during the last Ice Age. This species was native to the Pacific coast of North America. It is believed to have had small 'fangs' protruding from the tip of the snout and the adults could grow up to nine feet in length.

469 **The buthidae is the largest family of scorpions.** One of its members was tityus exstinctus. In 1884, the only known single male of this species was collected in the northern range of Martinique, France. It was concluded that the species had already gone into extinction at that time.

Scorpion Buthus (genus)

Kingdom: Animalia
Phylum: Arthropoda
Class: Chelicerata
Order: Scorpiones
Family: Buthidae
Genus: Buthus

470 The Xerces blue butterfly was a species of butterfly that was endemic to the Sunset District of San Francisco. It was the first of the butterflies that went into extinction in America due to habitat destruction caused by urban development in the country. The butterfly was last seen in 1943.

471 The bar-winged rail was a flightless bird native to Fiji. Though it was last collected in 1890, its last unconfirmed sighting is said to have been made in 1973. The bird is believed to have now gone into extinction due to the introduction of predators like mongoose and cats to the island.

472 The black-fronted parakeet is also known as Tahiti parakeet. It was found on the Pacific island of Tahiti. In 1844, Lieutenant des Marolles collected its last specimen. The birds were kept as pets by many, but ultimately became extinct after the introduction of cats and European rats in the area.

DETAILS OF EXTINCT ANIMALS

473 **Mekosuchus was an extinct reptile belonging to the species of crocodiles.** It was common in the South Pacific and France. It is believed to have become extinct after the arrival of humans on the South Pacific islands, around 1,000 BC.

474 The choiseul pigeon, which is also known as the Solomon crested pigeon or the Solomon Island crowned-pigeon, was a species of bird related to the pigeon and dove family. It was found on the Solomon Islands and reportedly also might have lived in the nearby islands. The last confirmed sighting of the bird was in 1904.

475 Another species of bird that went into extinction was the Kosrae starling or the Kosrae Island starling. It resembled a crow with its glossy black colour, but had a curved beak and a long tail. Its last specimen was seen between December 1827 and January 1828. Its extinction was caused by the rats that became widespread on Kosrae during the 19th century.

EXTINCT ANIMALS

476 A species of duck that was native to the Mariana Islands was the Mariana mallard or Oustalet's duck. It became extinct in 1974 and the major reasons for its extinction were hunting and habitat destruction caused due to draining of wetlands for agricultural purposes and for construction.

477 Volia was a sub-species of crocodile that became extinct during the later Ice Age. It was endemic to Fiji and was only two or three metres in length. Though it was small in size, it was one of the major predators of its time.

478 The red-moustached fruit dove is an extinct species of bird that was endemic to the Marquesas Islands, France. It became extinct in 1922. The main reason for its extinction was the spread new predators such as the then newly introduced great horned owl and the introduction of rats and cats in the area.

DETAILS OF EXTINCT ANIMALS

479

The white-winged sandpiper, also known as the Moorea sandpiper, is an extinct species of bird that was found in French Polynesia. William Anderson collected two specimens between September and October 1777, but both of them disappeared and the species was ultimately declared extinct in the 19th century.

480

The Tanna ground dove or Forster's dove of Tanna was known to us from two specimens, both of which are now lost. The last known Tanna ground dove was shot in 1774. In the early 18th century it was declared extinct due to hunting and predation by rats.

481

The levuana moth was commonly found in Fiji. In 1877, the levuana moths became a serious issue of concern when they attacked coconut plants in huge numbers. They were reduced immensely in 1925 by a biological control programme, and are believed to have been extinct since.

EXTINCT ANIMALS

482 The kioea was a species of bird that was endemic to Hawaii. The population of the bird had started to decrease even before the discovery of the island by the Europeans. The kioea became extinct around 1859, but the main reason for its extinction is unknown.

483 One more extinct species of bird is the Lana'i hookbill, which was a species of Hawaiian honeycreeper. It was native to the island of Lana'i in Hawaii. The natives of Hawaii could not find any more of these birds, and it was declared extinct in 1918. Several causes led to its extinction including its habitat destruction, avian malaria, and introduction of feral cats and rats to the island.

DETAILS OF EXTINCT ANIMALS

484 The New Zealand quail was first described by Sir Joseph Banks when he visited New Zealand. The male and female quail were similar, but the female was lighter. The first specimen of the quail was collected in 1827, but the species became extinct by 1875.

485 The New Zealand grayling was a species of fish found in the lowland rivers and streams of New Zealand. During the 1860s their population began to decline, before they finally became extinct in the 1930s. The main reasons for its extinction were deforestation and competition from feral trout.

EXTINCT ANIMALS

486 The Lesser Mascarene flying fox or small Mauritian Flying Fox was a species of Bat that lived in the Mascarene Islands of the Indian Ocean, the islands of Réunion and Mauritius. However, forest clearance and hunting caused this bat to gradually die out and become extinct.

487 An extinct species of tortoise resided in the Réunion Island in the Indian Ocean, and is known as the Réunion giant tortoise. They were hunted and killed by the European sailors for food and oil. Introduction of pigs and rats also harmed the species by destroying their hatchlings and eggs until they became extinct in the 1840s.

DETAILS OF EXTINCT ANIMALS

488 Cuvieronius is an extinct mammal named after the French naturalist Georges Cuvier. It was native to South America and was 7.5 feet tall, weighing about 3.9 tonnes. It resembled the present-day elephant with spiral-shaped tusks. It became extinct around 4,000 BC.

489 The dire wolf is an extinct species of carnivores that were endemic to North and South America. This species was about the same size as the largest gray wolves. It became extinct during 11,000 BC. Climatic change, competition with other species, and human hunting were some of the reasons for its extinction.

EXTINCT ANIMALS

490

The Kona grosbeak was a species of Hawaiian honeycreeper and was native to the Hawaiian Islands. It was already rare when it was first discovered, and it was last collected in 1894. Since then it has been described as extinct though the reasons for its extinction are not well known.

491
O'ahu 'akepa was a beautiful Hawaiian honeycreeper that lived on the island of Oahu. It was last sighted in the 19th century after which it became more and more rare. Finally, in the 1990s it was declared to be extinct. This brick red coloured bird had a slight crossbill that helped it to open up buds when searching for nectar and insects.

DETAILS OF EXTINCT ANIMALS

492 Another Hawaiian honeycreeper that has become extinct is the Hawaii Mamo. It was nine inches in length and black and yellow in colour. It had a three-inch long curved bill. This beautiful bird became extinct because of habitat loss and over-collecting by humans.

493 Ground sloths have been extinct from North and South America for more than 10,000 years now. Studies have shown that their disappearance occurred shortly after humans inhabited their living areas. Some other researchers believe that climatic change had more to do with their disappearance than human hunting.

494 The archaeopteryx is believed to be the first-ever winged bird of our planet. It was a bird-like dinosaur. Unlike modern birds, the archaeopteryx had asymmetrical flight feathers and broad tail feathers. From its fossils, it is not clear if this bird was capable of flapping flight or if it was simply a glider.

EXTINCT ANIMALS

495 A fish species found in Lake Techirghiol in southern Romania was the Techirghiol stickleback. It was 2.6 inches in length and was a freshwater fish. In the 1960s it was seen for the last time, after which it was declared extinct. The main cause for its extinction was its hybridisation with the three-spined stickleback.

496 A species of bird found only in the Hawaiian Islands was the Greater Koa finch. These birds were already living in a marginal habitat, when the introduction of black rats that preyed on the birds contributed to the decline of their population. Avian malaria was also another cause for their extinction. In 1896, the last confirmed sighting of the bird was made.

DETAILS OF EXTINCT ANIMALS

497 **The glyptodont was endemic to North America and belonged to the family of large armadillos.** At the end of the Ice Age it is believed to have become extinct, although its lightly armoured and flexible armadillo relatives survived. Coincidently, the extinction of glyptodonts occurred around the same time as humans first appeared in America, and they seem to have made use of the glyptodonts' armoured shells.

498 **The ancestors of domestic cattle were the aurochs.** These were large, wild cattle found in Europe, Asia, and North Africa. The range of aurochs was decreasing and by the 13th century they were restricted to only a few areas near Romania. The last aurochs died in 1627 from natural causes, but the extinction was caused over a period of time due to unrestricted hunting, diseases, and narrowing of habitat.

EXTINCT ANIMALS

499 A sub-species of otter that was native to Japan was the Japanese river otter. During the 1930s, the population of this otter suddenly shrank and by 1979 it became extinct. Hunting of the species was one of the main causes for its extinction. Other causes were pollution in the rivers, causing destruction of their habitat.

500 There was a sub-species of moose called the Caucasian moose that was found in the Caucasus Mountains of Eastern Europe and some parts of Asia. The sight of this species was quite common until the mid-19th century when it drastically began to decrease and finally became extinct. Asiatic lions, leopards, Caspian tigers, gray wolves, and Syrian brown bears were some of its natural predators.